This Is My Body

*A Memoir of
Religious and Romantic
Obsession*

THIS
IS MY
BODY

*A Memoir of
Religious and Romantic
Obsession*

CAMERON DEZEN HAMMON

LOOKOUT BOOKS
University of North Carolina Wilmington

First printing, October 2019
ISBN: 9781940596327 | E-BOOK 9781940596372

LIBRARY OF CONGRESS CATALOGING-IN-PUBLICATION DATA
Names: Hammon, Cameron Dezen, author.
Title: This is my body : a memoir of religious and romantic obsession / Cameron Dezen Hammon.
Description: Wilmington : Lookout Books, University of North Carolina Wilmington, 2019.
Identifiers: LCCN 2019025998 (print) | LCCN 2019025999 (ebook) | ISBN 9781940596327 (paperback) | ISBN 9781940596372 (ebook)
Subjects: LCSH: Hammon, Cameron Dezen. | Singers—United States—Biography. | Contemporary Christian musicians—United States—Biography. | Christian life—United States.
Classification: LCC ML420.H1236 A3 2019 (print) | LCC ML420.H1236 (ebook) | DDC 818/.603 [B]—dc23
LC record available at https://lccn.loc.gov/2019025998
LC ebook record available at https://lccn.loc.gov/201902599

"How Great Thou Art". Words: Stuart K. Hine. Music: Swedish folk melody/adapt. and arr. Stuart K. Hine. Copyright © 1949, 1953 The Stuart Hine Trust CIO. USA, North, and Central American print rights and all Canadian and South American rights administered by Hope Publishing Company. All other North and Central American rights administered by The Stuart Hine Trust CIO. All rights reserved. Used by permission of Hope Publishing Company.

The lines from "Diving into the Wreck". Copyright © 2016 by the Adrienne Rich Literary Trust. Copyright © 1973 by W. W. Norton & Company, Inc. from *Collected Poems: 1950–2012* by Adrienne Rich. Used by permission of W. W. Norton & Company, Inc.

The line from *Bluets*. Copyright © 2009 by Maggie Nelson. Published by Wave Books. All rights reserved. Used by permission of Wave Books.

Lyrics from "Mended". Written by Latifah Alattas (SESAC) Moda Spira Publishing and David Cameron Wilton (BMI) A Boy and His Kite. Used by permission of Latifah Alattas.

Lookout Books gratefully acknowledges support from the University of North Carolina Wilmington.

LOOKOUT BOOKS
Department of Creative Writing | University of North Carolina Wilmington
601 S. College Road | Wilmington, NC 28403 | lookout.org

"This fearless examination of Cameron Dezen Hammon's dark night of the soul begins with a startling moment, where death and sex and God and doubt swirl around each other. Then, word by word—slowly, beautifully, thrillingly—she circles that moment, until a hard-won mercy emerges."

—**NICK FLYNN**, author of *The Reenactments*

"Fundamentalism has a way of reducing all of life's complexities into a rigid set of binaries—pure or impure, sinner or saint, saved or damned. In *This Is My Body*, Cameron Dezen Hammon chronicles her initial love affair with the evangelical faith, her gradual discomfort with its patriarchal structures, and her brave pursuit of a more nuanced spirituality. Hammon's prose soars as she boldly dismantles the rigid worldview that once gave her comfort and rebuilds from the ground upwards, newly committed to authenticity and truth. Unflinchingly honest and searingly lyrical, this is a song of a book."

—**JESSICA WILBANKS**, author of *When I Spoke in Tongues*

"To find answers, Hammon must find the questions. And then she must persist in asking them. What we learn from this book is that it is human to love, and it is human to need to be loved."

—**ANGELA MORALES**, author of *The Girls in My Town*

"With honesty and courage, Cameron Dezen Hammon confronts the personal, the spiritual, and the cultural in this stunning memoir. Written in sharp and lucid prose, Hammon explores passion, doubt, and the risks of faith. *This Is My Body* carries an urgency and a candor seldom seen in contemporary memoirs. In two words, Hammon's story is beautiful and brave."

—**MARK HABER**, Brazos bookseller and author of *Reinhardt's Garden*

"When one rests in the truth of their own story, it allows all those who hear that truth to find their own rest. I rested deeply in the truth of *This Is My Body*. And that truth set me free."

—**SCOTT ERICKSON**, author/artist of *Prayer: Forty Days of Practice*

For MPH

What is it we want when we can't stop wanting?

—CHRISTIAN WIMAN

CONTENTS

Author's Note

Memoir is almost entirely a work of memory, and memory is imperfect. I have conducted interviews, but most of what I've recorded here is what I was able to recall myself.

I've used three different translations of the Bible: the New International Version, the King James Version, and the English Standard Version. I used the NIV in instances when I wanted to represent the text I was using at the time, the KJV when I wanted a more poetic translation, and the ESV when I thought it expressed the intent of the passage with the most clarity.

Most of the names of the people in this book have been changed, along with some identifying details. With the exception of St. Mark's, all names and locations of the churches I mention have been changed. A few scenes and characters have been compressed for clarity and readability. Everything else is as true as I could make it.

Dead Girls

My phone buzzes in the pocket of my dress. I slip my hand in to silence it. "I wish I could hold you." The text message is from a man I've given no name to in my contact list. Whose number I've blocked and unblocked in turns. A man I was with just one week ago, a man I might love, who is not the father of my eight-year-old daughter. Not my husband of twelve years.

From where I stand on the stage, I can see only the back of the open casket. I fidget with my dress and glance around the room as the spotlight slowly comes up over me. The stage is four feet off the ground, deep and long, with a floor-to-ceiling screen behind it flanked by two more illuminated screens. The Refuge, this suburban megachurch, meets in a converted gymnasium. During the week, the gym is used for youth-group basketball games. Darkened as it is now, with an elaborate lighting trellis that soaks us in purples and blues while projecting geometric patterns onto the walls, it looks like a set from *Tron*. The blue lights make the white casket lid glow. Smoke billows from stage left, and the band strikes a minor chord. The music swells behind me, and I open my mouth, ready to sing, but try not to make eye contact with the bereaved family weeping in the front row. My husband stands just to my right, strumming his acoustic guitar. I wrap my hand around my phone, now silent in my pocket.

I've been on staff at this church as a worship leader—a paid singer and bandleader—for about a year, and the sound-and-light show is part of every regular service we do, one on Saturday night and two on Sunday morning. I've been a singer all my life, but a Christian singer for just over ten years—at a Presbyterian church with ruby-red carpeting, an Episcopal church that boasted George H. W. and Barbara Bush as members, and an edgy downtown nondenominational church that met in a converted warehouse. Pushing forty now, I know that the preference in a church like this is for a younger woman to do my job, to help draw in other young people. But I tend to look younger than I am, and I make it a point to dress like the millennials the church hopes to attract. I think this is part of why they hired me. The man who texted me is younger than I am by a few years. We type things like "wywh" (wish you were here) and "omw" (on my way) in our exchanges sometimes, a nod to the irony and impossibility of our situation. I glance at my husband, whom I love, but whom I've felt distant from for years. He's looking out over the silent congregation as the rest of the stage lights come up. I begin the first song, let the notes slide from my throat. The wireless microphone picks up the slight tremble in my voice, the sip and rattle of my breath.

Despite my decade of experience as a minister, I'm surprised by this dramatic presentation for a funeral. Very often a grieving family, especially one in shock, will leave the details of the service to the pastors and staff. In this case, they've decided to produce a funeral much like any weekend worship service. Without the casket, a passerby might confuse us for a nightclub. When the church leadership, including the aging senior pastor and somewhat secretive committee of influential and generous laypeople, whom I've never met, designed the Refuge, they did it with this goal in mind. But I'm not sure they anticipated that the flashy aesthetic would extend to funerals. Other buildings on the church's sprawling campus are more traditionally reverent, with wooden pews and stained glass.

The young pastor of the Refuge is a recent seminary grad, a transplant to Texas from Florida, and this is a high-stakes job for him. Since he arrived a few months ago, he's been aggressively trying to address the church's dwindling attendance and increase membership, an unstated but clear expectation. If he's unable to, it's likely he won't keep his job for long. Maybe he recommended the family hold the funeral in this space, a way to show grieving friends and loved ones the spectacle that is the Refuge, to create a captive audience that might otherwise never venture through its doors.

The young woman in the casket is a recent high school graduate who flipped her car into a ditch on her way home from a party a few nights ago. Her family had attended the Refuge only a few times, but when news of her tragic death reached the young pastor, he was more than willing to host the funeral. Though never said outright, it's understood that a tragedy like this can bring a family back into the fold.

I watch for my cue to start the next song, a line of lyrics

that will appear on the hidden monitor by the sound board. I've selected songs—a mix of hymns and contemporary Christian songs—for their contemplativeness, and also for the way they frame the promise that true believers, once they pass over into death, will be restored in their bodies, in full, shining health. The young pastor—who has cool tattoos and a ponytail—has written a sermon that he will deliver from memory, and I can see from his trembling shoulders that he's nervous. He's new to this big-production style of church, just like I am. Even after a year, each service still feels like a sequence of unnatural choreography that I keep forgetting. The technical director, who oversees production with a walkie-talkie and in-ear monitor like a Broadway stage manager, has been at the church the longest, and even she seems out of her depth. The sound and lighting staff and me—we've all done funerals before, but not funerals in this space, and not for someone so young.

So we do what we're here to do. We put on a show.

When I arrived earlier in the day, I came in through the main Refuge entrance rather than through the backstage greenroom, which requires an electronic security card I'd forgotten at home. It is an important part of the church's elaborate security policy, designed to protect the hundreds of thousands of dollars in audiovisual equipment stored there, but I think it's absurd to require a security card to get into a church and often forget it. I had found the Refuge empty except for the casket and the hundreds of folding chairs that had been set up in anticipation of a large crowd. I looked away quickly but not quickly enough, not before I saw blue lights on her skin, blond hair stiffly arranged on a white satin pillow.

Looking down from the stage now, I think of my daughter, who's with her grandparents today. She has blond hair too, though I'm dark haired and dark eyed. I see her long, thick hair on that pillow and shudder. A wave of guilt follows for the thought of her in this moment, with my hand on my phone, anticipating the next message from the man I might love. I try to return my thoughts to the casket, to the beautiful young girl inside. I've always thought having an open casket was strange, but I recall something I read once about its religious purpose. It's meant to draw attention to the absence of the spirit, the animating quality that is unrepeatable, so totally unique to each person—absence painfully evident when a dead body is on display. The open casket is meant to make viewers wonder about the spirit itself, where the spirit has gone.

The eighteen-year-old girl grew up here, in Greenhills, a bedroom community forty miles outside of Houston. Forty miles on the hot, winding interstate that leads into the affluent suburb. It's the kind of planned community that has gated subdivisions built around golf courses and two shopping malls within a block of each other. It was founded in 1983 by a real estate developer who wrestled the overgrown land into methodically divided plots—plots that would attract a conference center, luxury homebuilders, and, eventually, multinational oil companies.

It's hard for small businesses to thrive here, but on every other corner, one can find a Cheesecake Factory or a church. Like its neighbor Houston, which one study estimates is the most likely place in America where one might become born again, Greenhills is a majority Christian city. Churches own hundreds of acres of some of the city's most valuable property. They run state-of-the-art buildings that house schools, health clubs, and restaurants, and employ thousands. Very few people in Greenhills are poor or brown or lack the letters that indicate advanced degrees after their names. There are

plenty of churches with more diverse congregations in surrounding communities, but those churches can't afford to
offer me health insurance.

The local high school, from which the eighteen-year-old
girl graduated a few months earlier, has produced Olympic
athletes, Broadway performers, and nationally recognized
scholars. It is, unsurprisingly, brutally competitive. Kids
overdose, or drop out, or slide into averageness despite their
parents' intense efforts to steer them otherwise. Though a
youth-group dropout, this young woman was best known for
being a loyal friend, and for her beauty.

One of today's speakers is a volunteer with the Refuge's
youth group. She'll talk about the young woman's sweet
smile, her bubbly personality. The volunteer will conclude
her remarks by describing the girl's salvific moment, the
moment many in the congregation will be wondering about.
The question of a person's salvation is central to most of the
religious, Southern funerals I've participated in. It's a rhetorical question, at least in this context; it would be indel-
icate to wonder aloud if the girl was saved. Yet we need to
know, because the Refuge's foundational theology, Wesleyan
theology, holds that salvation can be achieved only through
ongoing faithful commitment to God, meaning salvation can
be lost by ignoring, renouncing, or forgetting God, as some
teenagers are prone to do. The volunteer's testimony will os-
tensibly answer the question we are too afraid, or too polite,
to ask. Then we can proceed to the most important part of
the service, where we try to comfort the family and ourselves
with what we believe is promised to the girl as a result of
her salvation. It's the promise I've chosen the songs around.
There is no real comfort for this grief—grief I can see on her
loved ones' anguished faces—but these are the moments
when the point of religion, of all religion, is clear to me.

In the twenty-foot-tall images of her on the screen behind me, she is tanned, wearing aviator sunglasses and sitting on the back of a horse, her long hair flying. Then she's in knee-high boots and jeans, ready for fall. She poses with her arm slung around a friend in the high school cafeteria, smiling, her kind blue eyes accented with dark liner. She's at a homecoming game wearing a Texas-sized boutonniere, what's called a homecoming mum, designed by her date and decorated with streamers in the colors of the college he'll be attending in the fall. These happy moments represent important milestones in a young life, but projected on the giant screens like this, lights flashing, they take on a strange effect. I know there's more to this girl than what we're seeing, a more complicated life, but the production choices obscure her.

I'm projected onto those two additional screens that flank the stage, the high-definition camera tucked behind the sound board mercilessly trained on my face. Do I look appropriately sad? Are the cameras picking up the crow's-feet, the parenthetical lines around my mouth? At the Refuge, the expectations placed on my physical appearance are a study in paradox. I should look young, but not too young. I should look pretty, but not too pretty. A pastor once advised that if a piece of clothing gave me pause—Did it reveal too much skin? Was a skirt too short? A top too revealing?—I shouldn't wear it. *Do not cause another to stumble*, he said with the slightest wink, quoting a passage from the book of Romans. We're both objects in this space, the eighteen-year-old girl and me, two different kinds of painted dolls. We are lit and arranged and positioned to scaffold the belief that women are to be seen in specific, prescribed ways. Even if, as in my case, we are also to be heard.

The tattooed pastor closes the opening prayer with a dramatic pause before saying "Amen," and the mourners shift audibly in their summer dresses, their too-tight suits. Jewelry clinks, heels click on the polished floor. *Safety pin me to your chest, so I can stay put,* I sing. *Please don't leave me in this mess, 'cause I am this close to unraveling.* My friend Latifah Alattas wrote this song, "Mended," and I've sung it at the Refuge before. In his meeting with the girl's family to plan the service, the pastor suggested it. When, later, he told me he'd done so, I cringed. I love the dark, driving melody and rhythmic pulse of "Mended," but I thought the lyrics were inappropriate for the funeral, especially the chorus: *Don't give up on me now, this can all be mended. We can iron this out, it can all be mended.* I wonder if this choice is another example of what happens when a grieving family is too exhausted to second-guess a pastor's suggestion. Of course all cannot be mended for the girl in the casket, not in the way we wish it could be, but this song is not about bodily mending. That's why I came around to it, why I'm singing it now. The song articulates that promise we are here to remember and be comforted by. I pull my eyebrows together and close my eyes as I sing, an expression of meaningful reflection, an expression I practice often. I wrap my fingers around the microphone stand. It's an old trick. If I'm holding on to something, the congregation can't see me shake.

There was a time I shook when I sang in church—a chill would pass through me and my teeth would chatter—and it was not from nerves. The sort of music I'd written and performed before my conversion to Christianity was angsty folk-pop, confessional four-chord piano ballads I played in coffeehouses and small clubs. When I began singing religious music in earnest, it was so different from the slightly ironic, post-grunge songs I'd written in my early twenties. The shudder I felt when singing in church was not forced or practiced but a mirror of something, the ache and longing

I felt for God, and for the people I thought didn't yet know this God, people whose eternal salvation I believed hung in the balance. I shook back then because I felt, or I thought I felt, the movement of the Holy Spirit, drawing all of us to itself. My shaking was not a unique phenomenon. The name Quakers is said to come from the physical shaking that accompanies an experience of God's presence.

I refocus on the lid of the casket. I see the teenage girl's mother out of the corner of my eye, and I know that if I try to imagine what she's going through, I won't be able to finish the song. I remind myself of why I'm here—not to grieve but to allow her to grieve. I think about the next line of lyrics and strain to hear the congregation quietly singing along, their voices buried beneath the blaring volume of the church's sound system.

Much of the time these days, I don't believe what I'm singing. I don't believe the promises and assurances of the hymns and religious songs, the references to Jesus—divine yet human, a friend and Lord. What I believe doesn't really matter though. I'm here to provide a service, to do a job I'm good at. I might be unsure about my relationship to the faith, but I believe in making space for this family's grief, regardless of the way the Refuge has produced the funeral. I grip the microphone stand harder.

The shaking I'm doing on the stage now is not from grief, or spirit, but from fear. An irrational fear, maybe, that everyone can read my face, my trembling hands—not just my husband but the pastor, the girl's family, the more than six hundred people gathered in this blue room. A fear that somehow they know about the man who sent me that text message. Fear that though I haven't slept with him, not yet, they know it's all I think about. That they know I've betrayed my husband, and I've also betrayed God. I should feel remorse. Or grief, or guilt. I don't. After I sing the chorus, the fear lifts and I feel nothing. My lack of feeling takes shape; it has a presence, like a hand. If I allow it, it will push me. Off the stage, away from my life. Though I've not thought beyond the leaving, and though I can't see, not even faintly, what could be next, running seems preferable to doing nothing. As the music grows and the chords ring out, something familiar takes over. I finish the song, and then the next song. I watch myself sing as if from a distance. I catch a glimpse of my image on the screen to my right. Who is that woman singing so passionately? I listen to each word as it leaves my mouth, carried by the familiar music, and I think about the beautiful dead girl. I close my eyes. I know how to do this. I impersonate someone who believes.

Shells

Nearly fifteen years before the young girl's funeral, I have a dream that I'm baptized on the beach, and it comes true. In the dream, I'm standing on the beach on Coney Island, looking at the flat ocean stretching out to the horizon. The sea and sky are a seamless, silvery gray. My bare feet dig into the sand, and shells dot the beach—oyster, mussel, calcified rock. Everything is damp, glistening from the tide. I wade into the water and sink below the surface. When I come up for air, I have a feeling of deep calm. I wake from the dream with that feeling and it lasts for days.

I almost forget about the strange dream until my new

Christian friends suggest Coney Island as the location for my upcoming baptism. I should be dunked in the dirty Atlantic, they say, and emerge a new person *in Christ*. I want to be a new person. When we finally board the Q train for Stillwell Avenue, a few weeks after my dream, a summer storm rattles our subway car. The aboveground tracks are slick and sway in gusts of wind. Lightning cuts across the tops of squat apartment buildings. My friends look at one another, and someone makes a half-hearted joke about getting struck by lightning at my baptism.

I've become part of Tribe, a small house church that comprises a dozen or so twenty-somethings, multiethnic New York club kids who grew up in religious families but are trying to carve out a faith of their own, and a handful of formerly irreligious white girls, like me. We practice a non-denominational version of charismatic evangelicalism that favors contemporary music, praying in tongues, and belief in miraculous healings. We're creative and spiritual misfits, trying to build lives as artists without losing ourselves in the process. Trying to live for something bigger than art, bigger than New York. We attend Bible studies and worship services together in bars, homes, and coffee shops.

I've never been to Coney Island before, though I was born in Manhattan and have lived in or around New York all my life. Traveling to the outer boroughs like this, especially as far out as Coney Island, feels like a journey to another country. I don't think of the ways that my two-year romance with evangelical Christianity is also part of a journey. A journey in which I leave pieces of myself behind, mile by mile—my half-Jewish childhood, my liberal politics, my shelf of new age books and tarot cards, guiltless sex.

Out the subway window, the haggard Wonder Wheel promises thrills in blinking neon. Nathan's Famous beckons with its bright yellow facade next to the rickety, wooden Cyclone roller coaster. And then there's me, at twenty-six: aspiring singer-songwriter with an overgrown Winona Ryder haircut and an unfulfilling day job at a fashion PR company on Madison Avenue, about to embark on a new spiritual life. Coney Island seems like an appropriately dramatic location for my baptism, a ritual that will mark not only what I'm leaving behind but also what I'm gaining—according to my new friends, a lost part of my self, some essential innocence, the part disconnected from God. What better place to do that than in the shadow of a decrepit children's paradise? Maybe the last time I grasped a firm sense of who I was and wanted to be was as a sticky-faced child, led by the hand through theme parks like this one.

I grew up in a New Jersey suburb in a mostly Jewish community thirteen miles northwest of Manhattan. Because my father was Jewish and not my mother, and because Judaism is a matrilineal inheritance, we were not really Jewish, and we never joined a synagogue. My father wasn't interested in his ancestral religion, but I was. I went to shul with my friends every chance I got. I swooned over the lilting, minor-key prayers sung by the cantor in his robes and tallit; the tiny lace doilies on the women's heads; and on Shabbat, the syrupy-sweet smell of the Manischewitz wine and the delicately embroidered linens that covered golden loaves of challah. One Saturday morning, while my friends readied to carry the Torah into the service and I stood beside them, eager to touch the scrolls with the other children, I was pulled out of the line by my collar. A rabbi stood above me and told me to return to my seat. He'd figured out that I was not a real Jew. I wasn't much older than eight or nine, but the experience stayed with me. I was hooked, not on Judaism but on religion in general—on something so magical and important that I was forbidden from participating in it. A club that didn't want me as a member was the only club I wanted to join.

As I got older, I continued to observe some Jewish holidays and traditions out of nostalgia, but it didn't feel right. I was aware that Judaism was all but closed to me, or I was closed to it, and that exclusion was too much to overcome. Still hungry for spirituality, I discovered tarot cards and palm reading, crystals and astrological charts, white magic and Wicca. I read books on hypnotism and tried it out on my friends. In high school, an astrologer I visited told me I was a *super spook*, someone highly in tune with the spiritual realm, pursued by spirits. She said it like a warning but didn't elaborate, and I was left craving more context, someone to help me make sense of this gift and of my religious yearning. After my baptism, I'll hear Christians call the kind of new age spirituality I was practicing "the occult." It is no wonder I was so drawn to it on my journey, they'll say—many "seekers" become enthralled by "demonic imitations" of the real miracles and wonders of God.

By the time I reached my twenties, I was looking for a belief system that directly addressed my primary concern—the sexual and emotional minefield I was navigating as a young woman in New York. My new age spirituality had failed to do that. It was not only a religion I was looking for but a mentor, someone who understood the pull I felt toward spirituality, and its opposite, the pull I felt toward self-sabotage in my love life, toward men who were no good for me. Even better if that mentor didn't charge by the hour, as the past-life regression experts and psychics I frequented did.

By my midtwenties, about a year before my baptism, I was reeling from a few failed starts in the music business, along with other age-appropriate postcollege failures, like when I contracted HPV from a DJ I'd met while doing lines of cocaine at a bar on Avenue A. I'd been dating someone else at the time, someone I cared about, but he was on tour with a band, and I was lonely. Though I'd already begun to wrestle with Christianity by then, nothing had stuck. Left alone, my boyfriend out of town, I went home with the arrogant DJ, who pressured me into having sex with him. A crash from the drugs and a string of panic attacks followed, and then a month later I found out I had HPV.

I was suddenly vulnerable, a fragile physical body. I looked at my body, really looked—angling mirrors, crouching, and bending. How could a body that had brought me so much pleasure, joy even, turn on me like this? When I developed high-grade, precancerous lesions some months later, I decided that if I was going to die because of sex, I should narrow down my religious pursuits and choose Jesus, the only deity I had identified who promised an afterlife. I'd recently befriended a young British woman named Sabrina who'd moved to New York with her husband, Kevin, to start a small Christian house church, the church that became Tribe.

Sabrina and I began meeting regularly for coffee or beers, and walked through Alphabet City together while I asked questions. How could God be so good if his people were so awful? What about the Crusades? The Salem witch trials? "God is not the church," Sabrina said gently one afternoon as we ate veggie burgers in a café on St. Mark's Place. She flicked her blond bangs out of her eyes and said, "The church is made of people and people fail." Which made sense to me. Sabrina made sense to me—and she had what I wanted: a happy marriage at twenty-seven, a purposeful life, confidence about the world and her place in it.

A few months later, while we sat sipping white Russians in the bar at the Soho Grand after a wedding, Sabrina asked me if I wanted to pray. Right then, in the middle of the bar.

I was still new to Christianity, though I had the sense that my meetings with Sabrina were leading up to that moment. I was also still dealing with both the symptoms and the shame of HPV, but I didn't mention that. I didn't want Sabrina to think my conversion would be disingenuous, that my fears over contracting it were driving me. Maybe I myself didn't want to think that. If I could align with God as one aligns with a team or a nation or a political party, maybe that alignment could protect and help me. Sitting at the bar, Sabrina asked if I wanted to give up my past and *give God my life*. Would I let *Jesus into my heart?* More than anything, I wanted her certainty, her beatific calm. I repeated the words of the prayer: *Lord, I confess that I'm a sinner, that my sins have separated me from you. I believe you died for my sins and rose from the dead. Please forgive me and come into my heart so that I can live for you.* I was flooded with what I can most accurately call relief. It was as though the answer to a riddle I'd been trying to solve all my life had suddenly become clear.

Years after my baptism, a friend, a somewhat eccentric homeopath, will tell me that I suffer from the delusion that God is uniquely disappointed with me, that I've been singled out for *God's wrath*. A kind of religious hypochondria. This condition is so common, she'll say, that there's an herbal remedy for it. My HPV was also common, the most common STD on earth by some estimates, and could also be somewhat easily cured—another piece of information I'd make significant decisions in the absence of. In the shadow of the Wonder Wheel, my experience with HPV would feel utterly singular, cosmic even, as experiences can at twenty-six. I'd be ready to make an equally cosmic declaration to deal with it.

When I met Sabrina and got involved with Tribe, I found the religion and the mentor I was looking for. I abandoned my other spiritual pursuits for good. I stopped attending Seder dinners and Hanukkah celebrations. I no longer sat Shiva, the seven-day mourning period observed by Jews after the death of a loved one. I also stopped reading my horoscope, threw away my crystals. I ran headlong into Christianity— into prayer and worship, Bible study, volunteering at a soup kitchen. I learned old Christian hymns and songs and wrote new ones, plunking out melodies on the black lacquered upright piano I'd had since childhood. I stopped having sex—with my boyfriend, with anyone. I stopped donating to Planned Parenthood and let my Democratic Party membership lapse. I bought a copy of the New Testament and put away my new age self-help books. I began to walk the paces of what I believed was a religious life, a good life. I supplanted the rhythms of my childhood with the rhythms of the evangelical church. Maybe the person I should have been sitting Shiva for was me.

As the metal train wheels grind to a halt, the rain is coming down in sheets. We file onto the platform and under an eave. "I don't know how you pictured your baptism," Sabrina says, gesturing to the sky, "but maybe today isn't the day for this."

We watch the rain in silence for a few minutes, and to our surprise, it stops. We move toward the boardwalk with Sabrina leading the way, a clutch of bedraggled evangelicals, shaking out umbrellas, pushing damp dreadlocks out of our eyes, wrapping ourselves in faded beach towels. The sky looks scrubbed, wrung out, and flattened. A pair of drenched men stand by the wooden steps that connect the boardwalk to the beach. Candy wrappers, banana peels, crushed Bud Light cans are strewn like a tide has gone out and left the contents of a hundred garbage cans behind. The ocean is gray and flat. No waves. Aside from the two huddled men, the scene is nearly identical to my dream. "Hey, girl," one of them calls to me. I blush and look down. "Where *you* going?" He laughs, throwing his head back to expose a flash of gold-capped tooth, a tattoo of something—a spider? a snake?—crawling up his neck. We march past them, though I think his question is a good one. I want to turn around and run, rethink this whole endeavor.

When we finally reach the water, I kick off my flip-flops. Shells, rocks, and glass litter the sand. Just like my dream. Prophetic dreams are an important part of some Christian worldviews—the belief that God communicates to the faithful through dreams, through images and symbols. Ancient biblical prophets dreamed of impending doom, or they dreamed of a way out of a predicament. Throughout the scriptures, God speaks to people through dreams. I will learn this two years later in a women's-only Bible study in a Houston megachurch, but on this Coney Island beach I feel oddly comforted by the spiritual déjà vu. It is as if this place and time have always existed, as if they'd always been planned for me.

I look at the faces of the two women from my church who stand next to me in the sand—Sabrina, with her asymmetrical haircut and English accent, and Ella, a waifish grad student with a streak of green in her blond hair. Both are wearing tank tops and shorts like I am, modest clothes we don't mind getting wet, that won't become transparent as we wade into the ocean. Sabrina and Ella were complete strangers to me a year ago but have become my most intimate friends in a few short months. Sabrina tugs at the hem of her cutoffs. She looks at the water. "We'll have to get this done quickly, before the lightning starts up again." She smiles the smile of the preternaturally serene, the faithful, and motions for me to follow as she moves deeper into the cold sea.

My friends stand on either side of me and each grab hold of one of my arms, all of us waist-deep in the water.

"Cameron," Sabrina begins, "by choosing baptism, you announce to the world that you believe in Jesus Christ." She smiles. I look to Ella, who nods. "Do you believe that Jesus is your savior?"

"I do," I answer with a shiver.

"Do you trust in him?" Sabrina asks.

"I do." Ella gently squeezes my arm in encouragement.

"Do you promise to be faithful, to follow the one true God, to be his disciple the best way you know how all the days of your life?" The formality of her words make me want to giggle, but I don't. It's so different from how we usually talk about God, about everything. But it reminds me that what we're doing here is serious, that formal language has a place here if nowhere else in my life.

"I promise."

Sabrina smiles and nods. It's time. I close my eyes and hold my breath. I let my knees buckle, and I feel the cold water close over my chest and shoulders. Sabrina and Ella push my arms gently down until my whole body is submerged. I'm underwater for just one second, maybe two, the briefest instant. Then they pull me up to the surface, and I find my feet underneath me again. I gasp, air filling my lungs. I blink back ocean water. I'm a Christian now. I am *made new*. My friends from Tribe stand on the beach, beaming with pride. Some clap and hoot as we wade through the cold water toward them, toward their open arms and dry towels. I'm smiling so hard my face hurts. The sky is clearing, and, as if on cue, the sun breaks through the mottled clouds. I have a religion now, and a new kind of family. *Born again of water and of Spirit, washed by the Spirit and made clean.* Clean, finally.

It took less than five minutes.

You Must Change Your Life

A few months after my Coney Island baptism, I'm sitting at the piano in the sunny back room of my Brooklyn apartment, trying to write a new song, when I get a call from my booking agent.

"Are you sitting down?" she asks.

"Is this a trick question?"

"What are you doing next Saturday?"

"Nothing that I know of."

She laughs. "Good! Want to sing at the US Open?"

I've been invited to perform at a private celebrity party on the grounds of Arthur Ashe Stadium as part of the opening festivities. Yes, they will pay me, she says, and yes, I can play my own music. It sounds too good to be true.

"Oh, and they'll be sending a car for you."

I wander away from the piano to make sure that I'm not mishearing her, that it isn't a case of bad reception.

My musical ambition—my hopes for my first self-produced album, which I've just released—is intense, almost overwhelming, or at least it had been until my conversion. My new religion buffers me. It insulates me from the pressure I feel to do something significant with my music, pressure applied mostly by me. After a childhood of voice lessons, I auditioned for and earned a coveted spot at New York's Fiorello H. LaGuardia High School of Music & Art and Performing Arts as a vocal major. LaGuardia was the high school of so many successful artists—folk singer Suzanne Vega; the actress Sarah Paulson, my classmate; and, much later, Nicki Minaj among them. At LaGuardia, I focused intensely on a career as a performer, and it began to feel inevitable. But after college, I found the pursuit of musical stardom far more difficult than I'd imagined it when I was learning scales and singing arias at LaGuardia. It's been almost impossible to gain any traction in the music business, though I seem to be watching friends and acquaintances, other musicians I know in New York, score record deals. So much of this business is chance, being in the right place at the right time, things beyond my control. The call from my booking agent makes me think that this ineffable element—what I might have called luck in the past but now see as God's blessing—might finally be mine.

Three days later a white limousine arrives in front of my apartment, as promised, looking like something from a fairy tale. It will take me to the stadium, wait for me as I perform, and then return me to Brooklyn. My very own magic pumpkin. Later that night, after a somewhat shaky performance, I learn from my agent that Paul McCartney was sitting at the bar during my set. "Blackbird" was the first song I ever memorized, the first song that burned an impression on my child's conscious mind, that struck me with the power of what music could do. I didn't see Paul McCartney for myself—he was surrounded by a hedge of photographers—but I take his presence as further indication that God is for me, for my music, a sign of the *favor* I've been promised by my Christian friends, proof of God's goodwill. Paul McCartney as angelic messenger.

The person I want to call after the US Open gig is Matt, a soft-spoken, green-eyed Texan I am in love with, a professional musician I've been dating long distance on and off for three years. We are in an off phase, having broken up a few months earlier. Struggling with his drinking, he is also trying to reembrace the Christian faith of his youth, in part through his work producing an album for a young Christian singer-songwriter in Nashville. I thought Nashville would be an entrée into a professional and spiritual community for Matt. Instead it's another painful, expensive lesson in the cutthroat nature of the music business. He can't pay his rent or manage his drinking among Christian music executives who drink and drug heavily, despite their professed religious beliefs that emphasize temperance. Meanwhile, I'm becoming more and more zealous, leading Bible studies and getting more involved with Tribe, reevaluating my ambition, my career.

A few months earlier, in an on phase, he came to Brooklyn for the weekend, and we went out for a beer at my neighborhood pub. He'd driven thirteen hours from Nashville to see me, and I had the sense that his expectations for the weekend definitely included sex. But my born-again Christianity insisted on born-again virginity, and it was time to tell Matt that we had to stop.

"I'm a Christian now," I said, and took a sip of my Corona.

"We can't—"

Matt leaned toward me on his barstool, a half smile on his face. "But we *have been* since we got together," he said. "What's different now?"

"Everything is different," I said. "You know that."

The bartender looked over at us, then turned back to the taps to pull a pint. The bar was full of twenty-somethings from the neighborhood just getting off work. The jukebox was playing Radiohead's *OK Computer* in its entirety. "I want to get married," I said.

Matt nearly choked on his Hoegaarden. A big part of me thought that marrying a Christian man—this Christian man—could solidify something about my new faith and could protect me from myself. It was a necessary step toward the life I wanted. And I loved him.

"We're too young," Matt said, looking down into his pint glass. "We don't have any money."

"What does money have to do with it?" I asked. As soon as the words left my mouth I regretted them. I didn't want to convince Matt to marry me. I wanted him to want to. I straightened in my seat. "Whatever," I said. "Forget it."

Though he knew about my faith and I thought supported me in it, my desire for marriage and my commitment to abstinence in the meantime surprised him. Maybe it felt like I was withholding sex to get a proposal. Maybe he didn't think marriage was as important as I did. Whatever it was, we broke up not long after that weekend, and I stopped returning his phone calls and emails.

Even still, I know Matt will be thrilled for me about the US Open gig. I think that he alone, as a musician trying to make it, can understand my excitement. I want to call him, but after we broke up, Sabrina had put me on what she called a "man fast"—six months of no men, including Matt, especially Matt. She saw how upset I was, how fixated I'd become on him, and she thought swearing off men altogether would help me make more space in my life for God. I wrote a song during that time called "Enough," about wanting to end the cycle of ups and downs between us, about being willing to let him go if it meant an end to the pain of not having him in the way I wanted him. When I played "Enough" for Sabrina, she told me I could sing it as a prayer. She said that praying and singing could be one and the same. I should pray for *the man God has chosen* for me. If that man wasn't Matt, she said God would help me let Matt go.

Two weeks after my performance at the US Open, the night air is clear and cool as I ride in a taxi to Brooklyn. The weather has finally turned, the oppressive heat and humidity giving way to autumn. It's cold enough to suppress the dank smell of marine life that rolls off the East River all summer long, and I open the window of the taxi a few inches. My driver wears a red-and-white-patterned turban. His long hair is piled high and concealed by the fabric. I can see him from the back, through the dirty, fingerprinted Plexiglas that protects his ID picture and license. He's listening to AM talk radio, and it's turned up loud enough to rattle the speakers; the voices come through distorted. Over the Manhattan Bridge, the lit-up windows of warehouses throw slivers of light onto the river below. I'm on my way home from a party in midtown, an Interscope Records party where I sipped champagne and rubbed elbows with minor and major music celebrities. I want to tell Matt about this party, but I resisted the temptation to tell him about the US Open, and I decide I won't tell him about this either.

Despite still missing him, I feel hopeful about the direction my career is taking. The album I just released is getting good attention locally, including from the *Village Voice*, and I've booked shows at a few important venues. I inch away from the taxi's crackling speaker. I don't want my mood harpooned by the angry voices on the radio. A popular New York senator is talking about a suicide bombing at a railway station in Israel. He describes those killed—a woman, a young child, an elderly man, and others. I've never heard this kind of unvarnished emotion from a politician. His voice breaks as he promises swift retaliation.

I wince, hoping my driver isn't offended. Because of his turban, I assume that he's Muslim, maybe even Palestinian. I assume a lot about him, but I'm wrong. The turban he wears is an important aspect of Sikh religious culture, not Islam. I'll come to understand Sikhism as a monotheistic expression of Hinduism, but I don't yet know this. I don't know the difference between Sikhism and Islam, the presumed religion of the suicide bombers—a historically peaceful religion scripturally linked to Judaism and also Christianity. I don't know these differences because I don't have to. Since my baptism, though, and because of the oft-repeated biblical mandate to *go and make disciples of all the earth*, I've taken a keener interest in the religious lives of strangers. I've learned, for example, that in order to evangelize nonbelievers like my taxi driver—to share Christianity with non-Christians in the hope of converting them—I'll have to learn about their customs and belief systems, a task made more difficult when a person's religion has been insulted by the rhetoric of self-righteous politicians.

My own background, what I see as a kind of secular Judaism, doesn't seem to trouble my Christian friends. On the contrary, it's met with strange enthusiasm. Jews are *the chosen people of God*, they say. *Jesus was a Jew*—a refrain I'll use myself when trying to explain my conversion to my father. In the years to come, in Southern evangelical churches, I'll encounter a fetishistic fervor not for Judaism generally but for Jewish Zionism specifically. Israel, a place I've never been, is a crucial component of evangelical eschatology—beliefs about the last things, the end-times. Many American evangelicals believe that in order for Jesus to return, to judge the world and usher in a thousand-year reign of peace, Israel must be protected and kept sovereign at all costs. Otherwise, Jesus will have nowhere to return to. It occurs to me that if God were God of *all* people—Muslims and Jews, and everyone else for that matter—we should all be acknowledged as chosen. But, as I'll come to learn, Christianity is built on exclusion in many ways, on the belief that Christians inherit this status through Jesus, and only through Jesus can others partake of it. Special dispensation is made for Jews because Israel plays a key role in a cosmic battle over the Holy Land. Over the past forty or so years, conservative Republicans have leveraged these ideas into foreign policy that condones what I see as the unconscionable and violent repression of Palestinians. They've turned support for Israel into a dog whistle for evangelical voters, who choose to turn a blind eye to that repression.

My Jewish heritage will make me representative of a connection to Israel to some I will meet. It will grant me unearned favor in their eyes. They'll call me a *completed Jew*, a term I'll later realize is anti-Semitic and supersessionist. I'm one of the 144,000 Jews prophesied in the book of Revelation to choose Jesus during the end-times, and my conversion proves to them that we're inching closer to that longed-for final chapter, a new heaven and a new earth.

Even as a new Christian, these complicated ideas make

me uncomfortable. I don't believe that my Jewish heritage makes me any more beloved by God than my Muslim neighbors. I support Israel's right to exist and prosper in peace and safety, but I don't support the truly unholy political bargain struck between conservative evangelical Christians and the Republican Party. Still, it's a subject I'll fear is too sensitive, too potentially volatile, to bring up among evangelical friends. I'll worry that I'm too ignorant and inexperienced to understand the theology. Eventually, I'll come to see it for what it is—indefensible racism—but it will be years before I'm confident enough to express anything resembling outrage, or even the discomfort I feel in the taxi.

I meet the eyes of the driver in the rearview mirror. I imagine asking him about his religion, about the significance of the turban he wears. I imagine telling him that Jesus is *the way, the truth, and the life*, but I still have a hard time saying "Jesus" aloud with sincerity. I'm adjusting to these new beliefs, gingerly holding the words in my mouth like the first words of a new language. I look out the window, down at the dark water of the East River. I think of Matt. It's been weeks since we've spoken. I wonder if he's going to church, if he's praying. I wonder if he's met someone else.

I don't talk to the taxi driver. I don't know how to. I know only that Jesus is in my heart, has given me new life, a thrilling second chance. Soon, I'll be confident enough in the language of the faith to share it with strangers, friends, family. With anyone who'll listen. I look back at the Manhattan Bridge behind us, teeming with taxis and trucks, lowriders and minivans.

The World Trade Center is in my periphery now, always in my periphery, two silver columns shining from across the river. I pull my sweater around me tighter, press the button to roll up the shuddering window. It's colder than I realized.

The next morning, I have a hard time dragging myself out of bed. It's after 9:30 by the time I leave for work. As I walk up Fourth Avenue to catch the N train to Manhattan, fire trucks roar past me, their sirens wailing. I walk past Green-Wood Cemetery and hold my breath—an old superstition. I peer through the cemetery's metal gate and try to pray. A pigeon pecks at a bit of trash at my feet. More fire trucks. One, then another, and another. "I give you my life," I say aloud, startling myself. "I give you my life," I repeat. This is a more personal version of the prayer of salvation I'd prayed with Sabrina. I comprehend the surrender implicit in it now, maybe because I've put it in my own words. I'd been so eager to pray with Sabrina when I thought I could die from HPV. I now know I won't die from it—I've had a surgical procedure to remove the offending cells and was reassured by my doctor that with regular checkups I should be fine—but I barely heard my doctor when she told me because I believe it's God who has healed me, who has rewarded my commitment to him and made me clean, physically, sexually, and spiritually. To my shock, the dysplasia will return years later, necessitating another series of minor surgical procedures and causing me to fret, once again, over whether or not a sexual mistake will direct the course of my life and possibly my death. But standing outside Green-Wood Cemetery on the morning of September 11, I don't feel a hint of death. I feel almost invincible. I believe that God will protect my health, will support my music career, and whatever happens with Matt, God is in control. A line of scripture from the book of Jeremiah plays in my head like a refrain—*For I know the plans I have for you, declares the Lord...plans to give you hope and a future.* I feel like I did as a kid, closing my eyes, crossing my arms over my chest, and falling backward into the arms of a friend. Only this time it's God, this God I've only recently met, whose son's name still feels strange on my tongue, who will catch me if I tumble.

When I get to the subway platform, it's humid with bodies, a swaying, silent mob. More people come down the trash-strewn steps from the avenue, but there's nowhere to put them, no train to put them on. The mob edges closer to the tracks. The trains are backed up—it happens all the time, no big deal—though I've never seen it this crowded. So many people become one organism, like something aquatic, swaying in the breezeless underground. I wonder how many know God like I do—how many are believers? I think there must be at least a few of us scattered throughout, each of us a kind of sleeper cell.

A tall, thin man descends the staircase holding a news-paper over his head. "A plane flew into the World Trade!" he shouts. No one looks his way. He shouts again. Is he selling the newspaper? His voice and demeanor remind me of old-time paperboys, town criers. I pray again, silently this time. I finger a palm-sized Bible Matt gave me that I keep in my bag. The subway car arrives. Its glass and metal doors slide open.

I get on, and we're packed in here too—hundreds of us. An older woman with a sticky bun in one hand and *Page Six* in the other sits in front of me. When the train emerges from the underground, it stops dead on the Manhattan Bridge. I look out the finger-streaked window, squint, then move closer to the front of the car. The Twin Towers are burning. The woman looks up from her paper. No one says anything. She looks back at her paper. I think, briefly, Page Six *is a gossip column*, then *gossip is a sin*. I look out the window of the train car again, beyond the streaks, the grime, to the towers. I watch flames lick at the metal and glass hundreds of stories high, my mouth hung open. This fire is of a size and scale I've only ever seen in Hollywood films. It has an unrealness to it.

Though I can't feel the heat, the flames are so high and close it seems I should be able to. I wonder if the burning buildings are a protest of some kind, though of what? I wonder if it's somehow connected to what I'd heard on the radio last night—connected to Israel and Palestine. I don't think, not for a second, that there could be people still trapped inside. I assume everyone has been evacuated.

I make it to work, and moments after I arrive, the receptionist gets a call telling us that our building is being evacuated. *The Pentagon has been hit,* she says. We're a block from the Empire State Building. Could it also be on the list of targets? My coworkers and I run down the ten flights of stairs and file out into the street, to Fifth Avenue, where there are other groups of people gathered, staring and pointing downtown, in the direction of the World Trade Center. No cars, no traffic on the street. A few minutes later, around ten, I watch the South Tower fall from where I'm standing, hands clasped with the other women from my office. "We should pray," I say. I've never done anything like this before, never been so bold in public about my faith, but our current circumstances are unlike anything any of us have ever experienced, and I feel a strange sense of calm. We form a circle. I close my eyes and squeeze the hand of the woman to my right, who's crying softly. I say *help,* and *please,* and *God.* The North Tower falls. Fighter jets appear from nowhere. They're so loud I can feel them in my chest. Can we already smell the indescribable smell? Or does that come later? A one-hundred-story cloud of dust appears where the World Trade had been. "Amen," I say, and drop the sweat-slick hands of my coworkers.

When that limousine arrived to take me to the stadium a few weeks earlier, something shifted in me. An awareness of possibility. The weak presence of an unfamiliar hope that my life could turn, could change for the better. That this

God I'd claimed would show me his love by making my life easier, what I wanted it to be. Standing in the middle of Fifth Avenue, I feel another kind of shift. It's slight at first, like a tremor in a membrane. God will not make my life easier, no, but God will be with me in my life, as God seems to be with me in this moment.

I walk the ten blocks to my mother's building, where she's nervously pacing in front of the big picture window in her seventeenth-floor apartment. CNN is on the television. I call Matt, who is working on an album at a recording studio in Houston. I call and call, but it doesn't go through. It doesn't even ring. I can see the East River from that window. Fleets of ambulances idle silently on the street below. Bellevue Hospital is just a few blocks away. There are no survivors to fill the ambulances, and there will be no survivors to use the thousands of gallons of blood that will be donated in the weeks to come. I start drinking gin and tonics, one, two, three. As night falls, the old Pepsi sign in Queens lights up, winking against the clear sky. From this vantage point, it looks as though nothing has happened. Nothing changed at all. I keep trying to call Matt. By the time I get him on the phone, it's after midnight and I'm weeping.

"Oh my God. Are you okay?"

"Pray for me?" I ask.

Matt is silent for a few seconds.

"Hello?" I say.

"I'm here." I hear him inhale. Matt doesn't like to pray out loud, but I think he'll make an exception now.

"Lord, be with Cameron," he says. "Be with her...tonight. Please be with everyone in New York tonight." He pauses. "Please bring healing to the city." I can hear he's crying now too. "And please bring healing to us."

I tell him about the subway ride, about the burning buildings, about praying in the street.

"I want to be with you," he says. "I want to take care of you. What are we doing?"

"Do you mean it?" I ask. "I hope you mean it." I think of our conversation at the bar, how he deflected my proposal, how hurt I felt. It feels like a risk to believe he's changed his mind, but it also feels like everything that had pulled us apart before, all those concerns, are now insignificant.

"Of course I mean it. We should be together. We're wasting time."

"Where will we live?" I ask. He's silent. "Seriously."

"We'll figure it out. I love you. I want to protect you. I don't care where we live."

Though I know somewhere deep down that this idea of his protection is a myth, I believe in myths. The idea makes me bristle, grates against the feminist dormant inside me, but I think that this dynamic between men and women is another part of Christianity—like the strange ideas about Judaism—that maybe I'll grow to understand in time. "Nothing but what God wants matters," I say, haltingly, hoping that he will agree that God wants us together. I want that sense of rightness and ordained-ness to be understood between us, not simply to change Matt's mind. God wanting this is the only way I can justify what I already know will come next—leaving New York, my job, my church, my band.

"What are we waiting for?" Matt asks.

We begin to talk about a plan for me to move to Houston, where he's from and has returned to after packing up his Nashville apartment for good. Houston, that Southern city of hundreds of miles of junglelike vegetation and just as much concrete, steel, and glass. I think of the few times I visited there, its snaky bayous and hulking oil refineries, its manicured suburbs and fancy shopping malls. "It's inexpensive to live here," Matt offers. "At least it's a good place to start?" We speak on the phone several times every day for the next few days. I'm afraid that I'll lose him again, that he'll change his mind.

I tell Sabrina and her husband, a drum and bass DJ from the Canarsie projects, that Matt and I want to get married and that I am making plans to move to Houston. Because they gently insisted we all live in or near the same Brooklyn neighborhood, I can walk to their house from mine, and I've been doing that each night during the first weeks after 9/11. More often than not church members are gathered there to watch the news, to talk and pray—about the government's response, about the impending war, and about the ongoing efforts to locate victims. Though Sabrina and Kevin are hosting us all, as well as managing their own lives and emotional responses, they listen to me talk about Matt, about our plans. They pray with me and counsel me to be cautious. They're happy for us, though there are more pressing things on their minds.

By virtue of our identities as artists—not financial consultants or commodities traders—most of us in Tribe were nowhere near the Twin Towers that day, but we all know someone who was, or know someone who knows someone. On Tuesday nights, we read the Psalms aloud to one another and weep. We make lists of the names of the lost. A dear friend of mine from college is on that list. We ask one another unanswerable questions. Questions like *If God is good, why is there so much suffering?* And *Where is God in this?* The questions hang in the air between us as we try in turns to answer or avoid them, try to function as though functioning is possible with a mass grave just across the East River.

I think I know where God is. I feel a thick presence, not just in my life but all over the city as New Yorkers talk openly about God—on the bus, at the coffee shop, even in the newspapers. Because many of the first responders who lost their lives were Catholic, images of religious funeral services appear on television, are discussed on the radio, and, for a short time, talk of angels and signs and miracles becomes a regular part of public discourse. Though in Tribe our roots are Protestant and evangelical, the distinctions between Christians in New York become temporarily irrelevant. It feels like God is every-where. And it also feels as though I'm keyed into an import-ant religious conversation happening all over the city, about the nature of life, and death, and meaning.

A few weeks later, bleary-eyed, I walk past the handmade missing persons posters and makeshift memorials to a window-less room off Tompkins Square Park, where Tribe meets once a month for an event we call Big Hug. For our buildingless church, Big Hug is our equivalent to a Sunday morning service, only it happens on Saturday nights while the punks and Upper East Side socialites pack the bars on nearby Avenue B. When I walk in, Kevin has already begun spinning moody instru-mental electronica from his turntables set up in the corner. Christmas lights sag above him, and incense burns. The room, which we rent from a small missionary Baptist congregation, is wallpapered with handwritten prayers, newspaper clippings, poems, drawings, and photographs. A few members of Tribe shuffle around the humid room, stopping in front of an article or photograph to close their eyes and mumble a solemn prayer. Sabrina sits in the center of the room with several other women gathered around her—Selah, a petite, avant-garde singer-songwriter from Texas; Ella, the blonde with a green streak in her hair who attended my baptism; Chloe, a conservative account manager with bright blue eyes who once, in college, underwent an exorcism. Each woman touches Sabrina lightly, with fingertips or palms, on her forehead, back, or shoulders. Sabrina's migraines have often been the subject of our group prayers, not just at Big Hug but also on those Tuesday nights when we gather for Bible study at Sabrina and Kevin's house. She's suffered from them for years, but since 9/11, with the strange smell hanging in the air, her migraines have gotten worse.

"Sing, please," Sabrina says, patting the spot beside her.

I lay down my backpack and take off my headphones. Sabrina wants me to sing "Enough," the song I wrote about Matt and me after we broke up, when I thought we would never find our way back to each other. That's all changed now, so I have a hard time understanding why Sabrina wants me to sing it.

"You're saying 'Enough' to the pain," she says. "It's like...in a battle. When you sing, it's like you're coming to my defense, spiritually. You're interceding for me. Sing it over me," she says, "not to me." She smiles.

"If you want me to," I say.

I stretch my hand toward Sabrina as I'd seen the other women do when they prayed for someone. Kevin turns the volume all the way down on his turntables. There are about ten of us in the room, and each person is now facing me. *This is ridiculous*, I think suddenly, reflexively, as though the worn-down specter of my former, nonbeliever self has decided to make an appearance. Sabrina's head is bowed, and I can't see her expression. Maybe she doesn't believe it will work either. I look at Kevin for reassurance. He flicks his chin up toward Sabrina's bent head. I take a breath and open my mouth. *E-nough*, I sing.

My voice is small; I barely make any sound. It's absorbed by the room's ambient noise the moment it leaves my mouth. I swallow hard and try again. *I guess you want to see me*, I sing. *I guess you want to see me cry. E-nough.* The notes get stronger with each new phrase.

"Thank you," Sabrina says when I finish, and squeezes my hand. There are tears in the corners of her eyes. Kevin smiles, puts another record on. The tiny DJ light above the turntables illuminates his fingers as he sets the vinyl down.

Sabrina will ask me to do this again and again, to sing over her, or someone else. She'll introduce me to the idea that singing can be more than just entertainment or diversion—can serve more than someone's individual artistic goals. She'll show me that singing can be *worship, intercessory prayer,* the sort of prayer where the pray-er takes someone else's trouble to God on their behalf. I can see Sabrina's tightly knit eyebrows relax, the lines in her forehead smooth when I sing over her. I can see her shoulders sink, face slacken. I believe this ability is from God, must be from God. Is it Jesus? I don't know. I now believe that the sounds I make, what I can do with my voice, belong to me in only the smallest way. My voice is a gift, one I'm responsible for, something given to me on a kind of loan from God. I am its steward, and how I use my voice or don't use it has eternal implications. The thing I do, have always done, *sing,* now has a spiritual purpose.

This new way to look at music releases me, conveniently, from my battle with my own ambition. It reframes that ambition. Seeing music in the context of religion takes all the commercial pressure off it, at least temporarily, and allows me to see my musical endeavors through a different lens. Maybe I'm not selling records, but I can help people, like I've helped Sabrina. Singing like this makes me feel useful, holy, important—it's a feeling around which I will build my life.

A few months later Matt asks me to marry him on a dirt road in Central Texas while I'm trying to learn how to drive his stick-shift Volkswagen hatchback on a weekend visit. We're lost somewhere between fenced pastures and a herd of brown cows when he tells me to pull the car over and retrieves a ring wrapped in brown paper from the trunk. When I tell Sabrina and Kevin about the proposal a few hours later, they instruct me to pray. I've already prayed. I believe this is God's will, that *God is in control*, and I told Matt "yes" before he could even finish his sentence. Sabrina and Kevin happily give us their blessing.

After we call our family members with the good news, after Matt and I toast with champagne in plastic drugstore flutes, I pull my copy of *The Selected Poetry of Rainer Maria Rilke* from my purse, a book I've carried with me since high school. It will be some time before I break this old habit of going to poets for consolation and advice. It's a practice I'll later replace with Bible study, with *lectio divina*, but for now poetry is still necessary for me. I turn to the last line of "Archaic Torso of Apollo" and read, "You must change your life."

I begin the physical process of that change, packing, boxing, getting rid of. A lifetime of things sorted through, divided, discarded. I think of this move as making room for what's to come. I buy my ticket to Houston, Texas, to the Bible Belt, to begin again.

Tell You What He Needs

"I wish I could hold you." I save that text message longer than I should. After we return home from the teenage girl's funeral, after the long and silent drive back from the Refuge, Matt retreats to our upstairs bedroom to watch a documentary on Netflix. Our daughter, Sydney, colors on the living room floor, crayons scattered all around her, while I stare at my phone, waiting for the next message from the man I might love. A chill passes through me when the phone makes its familiar chime.

"Can you talk?" The air conditioner in our townhouse kicks on, a low, droning hum. It's hot, and the glass panes in the back door are fogged. "I'm here for you," he writes. "I want to be here for you." I'm sitting in my favorite chair, a blue tweed midcentury find I salvaged from a garage sale six years ago. I twist a loose thread from the cushion between my thumb and forefinger and consider my response. There's something delicious in this brief moment before I reply to him. I want to hold the reward of his attention for just a moment longer before the ball is lobbed back in his court and I'm the one waiting. It's a small thing, this pause. But it's a part of the game I'm playing with him, with myself. "I can't talk right now," I reply finally. "I want to, but I can't." Through our living room window, I can see that the grass in our narrow patch of yard is overgrown and being choked by dense south Texas weeds. If Matt's silence on the drive home and his disappearance upstairs aren't clues into his mood, the backyard certainly is.

The television is on, and Sydney watches it distractedly, a sitcom about a family with superpowers. The teenage daughter can see through walls, levitate. The son has superhuman strength despite his lack of common sense. Sydney laughs, and looks at me on my phone, then returns to her coloring. "Don't you have gas stations in Texas?" he writes. The man lives in another state, up north, but I know what he means, that I should make an excuse, get in my car, and go somewhere I can call him. We could talk and he could comfort me, presumably for the distress I'm in because of the funeral. It's not the cause of my distress, though I don't tell him that. I want him to think that it's the girl's mother, her friends and family I'm thinking of. But I'm not. I'm thinking of him. My head hurts; I pinch my eyebrows together and press my thumb and forefinger against either side of my nose to try to relieve the ache. I look at Sydney and recall the girl in her casket, her blond hair in stiff waves. "I can't leave my baby right now," I reply. He's silent, and the seconds drag into minutes. I know invoking my daughter, my responsibilities, will end our conversation for now. Does he understand that it's just for now? I have a life to protect, after all, the one I've been building for more than a decade. The TV blares a laugh track—the teenage girl superhero has just cracked a joke at her brother's expense and stands with her hands on her hips, rolling her eyes. The audience laughs again. I can hear the dull *scratch scratch scratch* of Sydney's crayon against paper.

"Who are you texting, Mommy?" Sydney asks as soon as I close the app on my phone, lay it facedown on the arm of the chair. How will I answer her? She turns back to her drawing, satisfied with my nonanswer for the moment. I see a grackle land on our fence, just outside the back door. Its black feathers glow blue in the sun. *What if he never calls or texts again?* I think irrationally.

Upstairs, Matt is doing what he so often does these days: watching television, playing his acoustic guitar, or surfing the internet while mindlessly petting our thirteen-year-old orange tabby, Steve. The air conditioner whines again, struggles to keep up with the August heat.

Matt has been out of work for three months. A year and a half ago he quit full-time church work and started teaching at a local high school. After ten years as a worship leader, he hated the way our music had been manipulated into something less tender, less authentic, and more like the soundtrack for a Christian game show. He took a chance, hoping he might really enjoy teaching high school, and he did. Teaching gave him the opportunity to distance himself from the all-consuming nature of the church—from the pressure to think and say and do the right things. To read the right authors and theologians (Bob Goff, C. S. Lewis), to listen to the right bands (Coldplay, Mutemath), and to watch the right movies and TV shows (*The Lord of the Rings*, *Lost*). Things that were hip and relevant to mainstream culture but suggested Christian values and ideals in a way that felt coded or subversive. Keeping up with it all had become its own full-time job.

In Matt's new job, there were other pressures. I'll learn that he wept in the men's room between classes that first year, the only way he could relieve the pressure of teaching more than 140 economically disadvantaged kids. I never knew how bad it was, how hard the transition was for him. I only knew that when he was home, he was unreachable. Despite his efforts to cope, Matt quit his teaching job and has been retreating even further into himself ever since.

I know Matt is prone to this kind of semiparalytic despondency when he's out of work. I first saw it when we were newly dating, after he got off tour with Bob Mould, legendary Minneapolis rocker and Matt's musical idol. When Matt returned to New York, where I was waiting for him to resume the relationship we'd started a few months earlier, he seemed distant. Before the tour we were falling in love, making out in taxi cabs, singing semidrunken duets together in my apartment on the East Side. But after the tour, when the money he'd made on the road started to run out—the "Mould money," as he called it—he struggled to replace it. None of the bands who wanted to hire him could afford to pay him what Bob had, and he could see no way to stay in New York without that income. He withdrew. He stared into space while I talked about music, about us, about anything. One night I suggested we look at an apartment in Brooklyn together. I thought it might pull him out of his funk. Our respectively held leases were a huge drain on both our finances, and I thought sharing that expense could relieve some of the pressure. The apartment was a typical Park Slope brownstone, beautiful and too expensive. We stopped at a bar afterward, and one drink turned into four, and a conversation about reincarnation turned into a fight about my sexual history.

"We just have to love each other," I said. "The universe is love."

"I think you've loved each other with a few too many people," he snapped.

Even though Matt hadn't attended church services in years, and even though *he* was a part of my sexual history, it appeared that his religious worldview about women who have sex before marriage—including me—had never really changed.

"How could you say that to me?"

"I'm sorry," he mumbled, and went to the bar to pay our tab. We walked back to his sublet in silence, and I spent the night as far away from his side of the bed as I could manage. I left before he woke up.

His comment could not have better met its target. I was trying to navigate the rocky terrain of being honest about my past while embracing new, religious ideas about sex and love. About what's right and good and what's not. I'd gotten the message from Tribe, from Sabrina and Kevin, that being honest, at least with God, was the way to let God begin to restore us from the damage we'd done before we knew him. I believed them. I didn't think God held my sins against me—I'd prayed and repented. I'd asked for forgiveness, and I believed I'd received it. If God had forgiven me, I didn't think the man I loved would hold my sins against me, the man with whom I'd committed at least some of those sins. Matt's comment made it clear, however, that it had somehow been my job to stay pure, and I'd failed at that job. The next morning, once I'd made the long subway ride to Manhattan from Brooklyn and had arrived at my office, I got a voicemail message from him.

"I'm so sorry," Matt said. "I'll never talk to you like that again. I know you don't believe a word of this," he said, "but I promise you."

Matt quit drinking for good soon after that night, but I

promised myself that I would not share my past, my sexual history, with him again. That I would lie if I had to. What I failed to see was that though the fight in the bar revealed something about Matt's religious views, it also revealed a lot about the way he handled the financial ups and downs of life as a musician. When he was flush he was happy. When he was broke, he was dangerous. At least emotionally.

We took a road trip to Austin together once, two years after the fight in the bar. We were talking about getting married then but were not yet engaged. In the car, flying west on Interstate 10, we listened to Patty Griffin's first album, *Living with Ghosts*, at our mutually preferred volume—deafening. We sang along together, and I watched the cows and trucks and hills of central Texas pass by from the passenger seat of his Volkswagen, the car he would soon propose to me in. When the song "Poor Man's House" came on, Matt got quiet.

"Man, that terrifies me," he said, turning to me, an unguarded look of fear on his face.

"What?"

He winced. "This song. I don't know. If we have kids, I mean. I'm terrified of being that poor man."

My upbringing had been more privileged than Matt's, and though I'd struggled with money as an adult, I had more of a safety net than he did. Because we hadn't talked about kids, and our engagement hadn't yet happened, instead of hearing the fear in his voice about money, about the uncertainty of trying to have a family when his ability to earn an income was so unpredictable, I heard only his desire for children, the admission that he was thinking about it. I was looking for clues that the proposal I was hoping for was forthcoming.

"Music," Matt said. "It's just not stable, you know? But it's the only thing I know how to do."

"We'll be all right," I answered. "God will provide." I put my hand over his on the gearshift.

I made the mistake of not taking his fear seriously that day. In the years to come, when Matt is working, he'll be affectionate and attentive. But when he loses a job, and then another, or when the unexpected expenses of life arise, as they so often do, he'll respond to that stress the way he had after the Bob Mould tour, just without the drunken explosion. He'll drift away from me. Get quiet. Disappear into a rabbit hole of online documentaries and music gear. I'll approach the glass, *tap tap tap.* Nothing. Then, when the circumstances change, when something gives—another job, a new album project, something that brings in steady income—he'll return to me revived. His humor will come back. He will become himself again. This has been our cycle for thirteen years.

I've signed off from that text exchange with the man, and I don't want to be alone with my thoughts. I consider going upstairs to Matt, starting a conversation. Maybe he'll close his laptop, set it aside. Maybe he'll open his arms and motion for me to climb inside them like he would've during happier times. Maybe I'll go upstairs and tell Matt everything. About the man, about my loneliness. Maybe if I tell him the whole truth it will save my marriage—or maybe it will end it.

I don't do any of that. Over the coming weeks, there is that distance in Matt, the familiar blankness. He won't hold me. He won't move the cat off his lap. He will often take long seconds to respond to my questions, my decreased attempts to start a conversation.

I believe, or I think I'm supposed to believe, that God will fix this. Fix us. Fix my loneliness, meet my needs. Or if God is not meeting my needs, then the fault lies with me. In our circle of friends—pastors, missionaries, music ministers—a wife's needs are just not high on the list of important things. Most women I know have an airtight veneer, one face for public and one for private, a duality cultivated over a lifetime of navigating evangelical communities in the South. *We're doing great! Bless your heart for asking. God is good, all the time.* Though I've never been good at the veneer, never skilled at adopting pious quips or posting biblical quotes to my social media feed, I'm not being any more honest about what's going on than they are.

Now, after the funeral, as I wait for the man to text me back, and as Sydney lies on the living room floor coloring and the cat sleeps soundly upstairs on Matt's lap, something is breaking down inside me. I have a taste of what it might be like to have someone who pays attention, who wants to know what I'm thinking.

Later, I'll tilt my legs back and forth, draw my knees together, cross one leg over the other, my shorts pushed up over my thighs, trying to catch the weak overhead light. I'll position my phone above my lap, higher. I'll take the picture. I'll take another and another until the disembodied legs in the image, so much apart from the rest of me, look the way I want them to. Look the way I think pictures of body parts sent by lovers who are unattached and free to send such pictures should look. I'll send the picture to him, though he hasn't asked for it. Not specifically. I hope the picture will give him pause, buy me some time. "Babe," he'll write. "Hon." He uses nicknames like this, pet names, names that feel far more intimate than we are. But I like it, and liking it feels dangerous. Maybe I like that too. I'm becoming tethered to him in a way I don't exactly understand and can't control.

"Get him to tell you what he needs," Roberta insisted, and "let him know his needs matter." A few years before the Refuge, Matt and I were hired as worship leaders at Faithbrook, a large, mainline denominational church outside Houston, in a wealthy, close-to-town suburb. They'd hired us to lead their struggling "contemporary" service, the service that featured a light pop-rock style of music that they were sure, if done properly, would attract the wayward millennials and Gen Xers who were leaving the Protestant denominations in droves. Faithbrook had hired a "church growth consultant," a former marketing professional from Los Angeles, a man who drove a luxury sports car and had never worked for a church. He'd suggested hiring Matt and me because we'd made something of a name for ourselves leading worship at a hip, downtown church called Koinonia, a church that had no trouble attracting and retaining young people. The church growth consultant thought we'd bring some of those young people with us when we took the job at Faithbrook, but the strategy had proven less successful than he'd hoped. Nonetheless, singing for Roberta's Wednesday morning women-only Bible study was one of the unstated expectations of my job, and I did it every week.

Roberta was well known at Faithbrook for making an unhappy marriage work. Her popular Bible study was packed with women who were also in unhappy marriages and trying to find a way to survive their unhappiness without dismantling their lives. Matt and I were unhappy. Though Matt was working then, our discontent was real. Sometimes, when we passed each other in the narrow upstairs hallway, he'd slam his shoulder into mine like a kid might do in the hallway at high school. I felt invisible to him.

During the opening session of the marriage class, Roberta confidently took the podium. She looked impeccable in her slacks and blouse, her hair freshly highlighted and styled. She said a prayer, paused dramatically, and looked up from her notes.

"Early in my marriage," she said, "I wished my husband dead."

She laid her hands on the podium and made eye contact with me, sitting in the front row, my notebook open and pen ready. The room was silent.

"I was unhappy," she paused, "and as a Christian I didn't believe in divorce."

She looked around the room at several women who I was sure either had been divorced or were in the process of divorcing. The metal folding chairs collectively groaned.

"And because I didn't believe in divorce, I figured the only way out of my marriage was if my husband died. Being a widow was okay, but being a divorcée was not."

No one moved. Though I had never wished Matt dead, I definitely understood Roberta. She'd felt trapped. Roberta loved teaching the Bible and was good at it; she had these women in thrall. She also loved the esteem she had in the eyes of the pastors and congregation. Like Roberta, I loved what I did. I loved being a worship leader. It made me feel important. We both knew that if we left our husbands, we'd likely be considered *unfit to teach* by Faithbrook's senior pastor. Teachers must be moral leaders—exemplary, at least in appearance. The performance of morality, more than perhaps morality itself, was what mattered, and *moral failure* was what they would call it if we left our husbands. If we strayed, or even if the men did. Roberta didn't say any of this that day in her Bible study because the few of us in the room who'd ever worked in ministry knew it intimately, knew the professional cost of this kind of "failure."

I could still remember the thrill the first time I stood on the stage of a church, the first time I sang to a congregation. What I'd experienced then was a change in how I saw myself and what I was capable of, of what I could offer with my singing, that sense of purpose I'd discovered in New York. People wept, raised hands, sang along. If my marriage failed, that would be over for good.

Roberta went on to explain that wishing her husband dead was a manifestation of her *sin*, a state of being we understood we were born with, a preexisting condition we inherit as human beings. Though we were all sinners, Roberta reminded us, her voice gaining power and volume, we didn't have to accept our sinful nature. We could make choices! We had *free will*! In the end, all Roberta's marriage needed was a little work and a willing heart. She had to *change her heart* toward her husband, she said. She had to *submit to her marriage, lay aside her selfishness*.

"He's completely changed now, y'all," she said in a stage whisper, leaning on the podium. "Just. Completely. Changed!" A chorus of *awwwwws* rose from the women. A few sniffled.

"And guess what," she added, pausing dramatically. "So. Have. I!" The room erupted in applause. Several women turned to their neighbors and smiled, assuring one another that they too could have changed husbands, and could be changed themselves.

I guessed wishing her husband dead was long ago; they'd gotten past it. But I knew by the casual way Roberta still described him to the class, the way she relayed something he'd said or done—not this day, but other Wednesdays—he probably hadn't changed all that much. She recounted brief snippets of their exchanges and she characterized him, always, as patient—with her neediness, her moods, her insecurities. But to me, he seemed unkind. Critical, aggressive. I saw something familiar in Roberta's stories, something I'd seen in the stories of other women I knew who were struggling in their marriages, or who had abusive partners. Women who didn't necessarily want to let on how bad it was. *He's patient; I'm lucky*, they'd say. Or *He's thoughtful; I'm a scatterbrain. He's generous; I'm demanding*. "Christian marriage is marked by discipline and self-denial," the German theologian Dietrich Bonhoeffer wrote. Most of these women were losing themselves completely in the process of trying to model that kind of self-denial. It's a setup for abuse and neglect, with a convenient religious motivation.

I wondered what would have been different in Roberta's life, in my life, if, instead of making the marriage work because it was our duty as Christian women, we'd stepped away from our unhappy marriages and gotten to know ourselves a little better. Would we have been able to form a romantic partnership we wouldn't have to force into this self-denial narrative, the narrative that was integral to Roberta's popularity among the women who attended her Bible studies?

Matt was not aggressive or unkind. He wasn't physically abusive. It would be some time before I understood that what he was—absent, distant, unreachable—had a name. Neglect is a form of abuse—ask any child of an addict or alcoholic. But at the time I wasn't thinking in those terms, and I wasn't yet willing to see my part in it.

Roberta insisted that we keep trying. *Buy some lingerie*, she suggested. *Ask him what sort of woman he would marry if he could do it all over again.* She led us through an exercise called Mail Order Bride, designed by a Southern Baptist preacher and author, a man, whom she often quoted during her Bible studies. In the exercise, we were supposed to fill out a questionnaire that detailed all the qualities we thought our husbands might want in a wife. Then we were supposed to take a clean copy of the questionnaire home to our husbands and have them fill it out. "Become the woman of his dreams!" Roberta said, passing out the questionnaires. I shifted in the cold metal chair and folded the questionnaire into my Bible. I couldn't imagine how knowing what Matt fantasized about, asking him to spell out what it was about me that wasn't enough for him, could help us. In fact, it made me angry. I thought it was troubling that a Bible study leader would endorse an exercise predicated on a euphemism for sex trafficking, something Roberta seemed completely oblivious of.

I looked around at the other women in the Bible study. A few sighed. "It's important that you show him that his desires matter," Roberta said. "Get him to tell you what he wants and try to meet his needs." *What about our needs?* I thought. *Our desires?* I'd never heard Roberta talk about that. Instead she taught us techniques to become better listeners (*Turn off your phone! Laugh at his jokes! Ask his opinions!*), better sexual partners (*Stop wearing old sweatpants to bed!*). Better versions of ourselves as partners, but not better versions of ourselves.

That night, while Matt and I were out on a date and Sydney was with her grandparents, I brought up the questionnaire. We sat across the table from each other, thumbing through the restaurant's heavy menus. Though I doubted Roberta, I told myself that she knew better than I did, that maybe God would use her to help us. I couldn't stand the silence between us; anything was better than that. When I asked Matt to describe what he would want in a wife if he could start over, I honestly didn't expect him to answer. Or I expected he would be diplomatic and describe me exactly as I was. *Someone to write songs with, to play music with,* he'd say, the things we still did together, the only things we really connected over. "I think I'd want someone who took pride in her home," he said, "and in her appearance. Someone who smelled good, who—"

"Who smelled good?" I shot back.

"No, I, I didn't mean—" Matt stammered.

I pulled the neck out from my dress and sniffed. "I don't smell good?" I smelled fine. I was clean. I wore deodorant, every day. I wore perfume. My clothes were newish. What was he talking about?

And our home? Where more often than not he was distant,

where he disappeared inside his own head. Where I had to beg him to change a light bulb or to take out the trash. Where I tried to keep up with the dishes and the laundry and all the rest of it. A burn of shame came over me, then anger. Maybe silence was better, after all.

"I need you to want me," I said finally. "If you don't want me, I'm going to find someone who does."

After we got home from the restaurant that night, lingerie was the last thing on my mind. "Should we talk?" I asked meekly, standing beside the dining table. He fingered a chord on his guitar and began to play. I walked away, into the kitchen to load the dishwasher.

Three frustrating years after Roberta's Bible study, the evening of the funeral, it seems to me that the man I might love understands my loneliness. He asks me questions and listens to my responses. He responds to the questions I ask him with more than one-word answers. His interest—*I wish I could hold you*—comes before I learn how to say *I need to be held*. I don't think about how far away he is, physically, because his messages are intimate, so close it's like they're whispers in my ear. Or like a voice coming from inside my own head, bodiless, always available. Like the voice of God. When I'm feeling low, or lonely: *buzz*—a text message coming in. Then a photograph, an email, a phone call. "Can you talk? I can't stop thinking about you. I need you now." Eventually, I'll learn that I'm not the only lonely woman he's messaging; my needs are not the only needs he's trying to meet. The night of the funeral I believe that I am, that what he is to me is worth protecting. I don't go upstairs to Matt, don't interrupt his Netflix. In fact, I hardly speak to him at all.

What would Roberta think of me now? I wonder. Matt upstairs in his own world, and me counting the minutes until I can text the man back. What would Roberta think of the photographs I've sent to him, of the things I've done and wanted to do? Roberta would offer to pray for me, to intercede on my behalf. Or maybe she'd tell me to pray, on my knees, to turn away from temptation and return to God and to my marriage.

I sit at my dining room table and pull out my phone. Sydney is drawing a picture: Matt as a stick figure standing beside her as a stick figure, a sun and clouds and trees. The TV is playing another show with a sassy female protagonist, the laugh track a constant refrain.

"How come I'm not in the picture, babe?" I ask, while finding his contact and opening a message.

She shrugs and smiles sheepishly but doesn't answer.

Tongues

Sydney is almost two, and we've just arrived in Budapest for a three-month mission trip.

"Could you prepare us some sandwiches, Cameron?"

The missionary leans deeper into the plush sofa and crosses his long, tanned legs. It's summer, and he's wearing surfer-style board shorts. I've been passionately describing the work I believed we could do here—the concerts, the suicide prevention outreaches.

"It's getting to be about lunchtime," he continues, motioning toward the kitchen.

Matt and Jimmy, the teenage boy from our church in

Houston who's come with us to Hungary, don't move from their seats. All three look at me with mild expectation. On the other side of the Danube, just a few miles beyond our borrowed mansion's big front windows, the city shimmers in a hot blur.

The word *prepare* is what catches me. It's a formal word, almost as if the missionary—who is an American—was translating one language into another and forgot the simple thing he's trying to say: *You're the woman. Get up and make us some sandwiches.*

The missionary and his family are longtime members of the church that has sent us to Hungary, Holy Immanuel, a fairly liberal, mainline Protestant church in Houston—one that ordains women and affirms them in leadership. Because of this, his comment catches me by surprise, and hot anger rises to my face. I turn to the lacy white curtains rustling in the afternoon breeze. Just beyond the French doors, potted pink geraniums soak in the sun on the white-tiled patio. Beyond that, the tennis court, and below us, the indoor pool. The family we're house-sitting for, also missionaries, has five kids, so they need a large house, and the temporarily favorable exchange rate had made this one—owned by a retired Hungarian soccer star—affordable to rent. It seems strange that missionaries should live in such opulence when most Hungarians struggle. My concern over the house has been blotted out in this moment, though. I have a new concern. I don't want the missionary to see that he's offended me. I don't want to drive a wedge between us on our first real workday here. I look in the direction of the kitchen and slowly get up from the throw pillow I've been sitting on.

A familiar wave hits—disappointment, embarrassment, shame. Disappointment because in Houston I'd come to expect the subtle and not-so-subtle misogyny of religious men, even in liberal churches, but in a major European city—a city I see as sophisticated and progressive, like New York—it seems out of place. The embarrassment and shame are harder to explain, even to myself. Once in the kitchen, as I rummage through the pantry, I replay the script I reserve for moments like this one: I tell myself that in this Christian life I've chosen, I need to accept the good with the difficult. *This is how we do things.* I tell myself that the work we will do here is important enough to weather a few blows to my ego. But having come all this way, having subleased our townhouse and moved halfway across the world for the summer to support this missionary's work in Budapest—I'd assumed he would be grateful, or maybe just polite enough, to see me as an equal.

The missionary's beliefs about the differences between men and women are not uncommon among white Southern Christians, even those in mainline churches that seem otherwise progressive. The denomination that Holy Immanuel is part of has been ordaining women ministers since the 1950s, but the influence of *complementarianism*—the theological concept that men and women are made differently, with different gifts, and meant to lead in different spheres—is still strong among some members, especially those involved with conservative parachurch organizations, or who came to Holy Immanuel from more conservative churches. *A woman should learn in quietness and full submission,* Saint Paul wrote in a letter to a young mentee, a passage from the first book of Timothy in the New Testament. *I do not permit a woman to teach or to assume authority over a man; she must be quiet.* Based on this passage, complementarians believe women cannot be preachers or pastors, not in the same way men can, and in all areas of life women should submit to male authority. *For Adam was formed first, then Eve,* Paul continues. *And Adam was not the one deceived; it was the woman who was deceived and became a sinner.* Complementarians believe that one of the consequences of Eve's transgression is the ongoing subservience of women in the home, in the church, and in society. Punishment that includes, but is not limited to, the pain of childbirth and the gender pay gap.

Holy Immanuel takes its views on women—at least on paper—from egalitarianism, the theological belief that men and women *are* equal. Church leaders see that passage in the book of Timothy as advice Saint Paul was giving to a particular church at a particular time, not as a blanket directive for how women are to be regarded for all time. In the denomination's doctrinal statements, they cite not the words of Paul but the words of Jesus himself. Mary Magdalene was the first person to see Jesus after the resurrection, an event recorded in all four of the gospels. "Go to my brothers and tell them," Jesus said as she wept in the garden outside of his tomb. If Mary Magdalene, and the apostles for that matter, had followed Paul's later instruction about a woman remaining quiet, the news of the resurrection would never have spread. Christianity is built on the witness of a woman—or that's how egalitarian churches see it. Holy Immanuel's denomination also ordains LGBTQ ministers, which is controversial, at least in the South, and exciting. Both the ordination of women and gay clergy are powerful signals that progressive values are influencing the church in profound ways. Holy Immanuel is the most progressive church we've ever been a part of.

And yet, it appears that missions—even those financed by our liberal church—are guided by a far more theologically conservative mind-set here in Budapest. The missionary sitting on our borrowed couch is still a member of Holy Immanuel, but he's worked for a conservative international missions agency that has been vocally complementarian for two decades. His views on women, at least as they apply to me, reflect that. Or maybe his theology was always conservative, despite his history at Holy Immanuel, and has been made more so by his time on the missions field. Wherever his theology comes from, it's begun to erode the zealous cloud of enthusiasm I arrived on.

In the kitchen, I attempt to make lunch while the men make plans for our next "outreach." The outreaches are to be the focus of our work here—Christian concerts we'll perform in the city parks, in the underground train stations, and at the ministry center, a crumbling building that houses the missionary's office as well as classrooms for Bible studies and English lessons. I have a lot of ideas about how we might approach the outreaches, mostly about what songs I think we should sing, and how we should share our testimonies so that they will have the most impact. My singing voice is part of the draw, after all, but I'm not offering my ideas and opinions. I'm in the kitchen making the sandwiches.

My enthusiasm about coming to Budapest was not only for the work we were sent to do but also for the opportunity to reconnect with Matt, to focus on learning new songs, and to prepare for the concerts we'll be performing. This work always brings us closer and reminds me that God blesses and uses our music. Our musical abilities are the main reason the pastors and lay leaders at Holy Immanuel sent us, why they believe we will be an asset to the missionary. Hungarians love art, music, and poetry, they told us, and God would use our talents in those areas to change their hearts and minds. To turn them away from sex, drugs, suicide, and greed, and toward Jesus Christ—an idea that is condescending and reductive at best but that the church's missions director, a petite but fiery Alabamian with a cloud of blond hair, sold vigorously. *Hungary is a nation of suicidal atheists*, she said. *In fact, Hungary's suicide rate is one of the highest in the world.* Other missionaries we'd meet in Budapest would corroborate her claims, telling us that suicide is a socially acceptable outcome for many young people struggling with the country's trio of social ills: unemployment, depression, and addiction.

Before I was sent to make lunch, the missionary explained that many of Hungary's national heroes—politicians and poets—took their own lives, and Hungarians trace this sad part of their history to a curse placed on them by the occupying Ottoman Turks in the seventeenth century. We believe that if the Hungarian people knew God, this curse would have no hold over them. If they knew the value of their lives in God's eyes, they would think differently about suicide. Our job is to show them that value.

I wholeheartedly believe in this mission. My previous life in New York—adrift, depressed, and atheistic—was not so different, I think, from those of the art-loving, cynical Hungarians. I believe they need what I have—faith and hope.

As I lay out the dishes, I feel suddenly self-conscious that I haven't yet washed the ones we used for breakfast. I hear Sydney stir in her portable crib upstairs; she's not crying exactly, just making the melodic babble that usually proceeds a crying jag. Just before the missionary arrived, Sydney had finally succumbed to jet lag, after two days of toddler hysteria, and taken her first nap. Judging by her escalating trills, though, the nap was short-lived. Sydney's toys—her stuffed animals and coloring books, her Barbies and the rubber-encased iPad loaded with episodes of *Barney and Friends* and *Caillou*—are piled up on the kitchen table. Crumbs litter the countertops, and a lone toddler shoe is wedged beneath a cabinet. I fear that I am not cut out for Christian domesticity, for the role of wife and mother, cook, cleaner, and caretaker. Or at least for the version of it expected of me here.

Before I had Sydney, I believed that motherhood would come as easily as Christianity had, an identity I could slip into and shape around myself. I believed that I'd float gracefully into the role of *mother*, as my church friends had all seemed to. But it did not come easily. Home from the hospital, I was consumed by Sydney's fragility, terrified that I would hurt her without intending to, that I was too clumsy, too easily distracted to be in charge of someone so helpless. When my friends assured me that babies are tougher than they look, I didn't believe them. Babies are vulnerable, all the books cautioned, and having one in my care, having to care for her with my postpartum body so slow to recover, made me vulnerable too. The stitches from my emergency C-section were raw and sore for weeks; they seemed barely able to keep my organs inside my body. When I tried to breastfeed, my nipples cracked and bled. When I tried to cook, even macaroni and cheese, I collapsed in a frustrated, sobbing heap. A mound of laundry sat in front of the washing machine, so in a moment of rare lucidity, I sent Matt out to Target for new T-shirts and underwear. I couldn't sleep. While Sydney slept, I'd lie awake staring at her, watching her chest rise and fall, waiting for her to need me. Several of my friends had multiple babies by then, babies they carried in organic cotton slings, sometimes one on each hip. Their babies were on strict eating and sleeping schedules, they "cried it out" if they refused to nap or sleep in their cribs. These friends were doing so well that it seemed effortless for them, and they tried to encourage me to follow a similar program. But I could follow no program. Sydney was my program, and she ate and slept when and where she wanted. I continued to lie awake at night worrying that I'd made a terrible mistake, that I would never cut it as a mother.

I was miserable, but I believed that if I prayed hard enough,

God would heal me, would turn me into the mother Sydney needed, the wife Matt deserved. I went to my Bible study group week after week with the same prayer requests: to sleep, to stop worrying, to stop fearing the worst, to stop my nightmares—recurring dreams where I forgot Sydney in the middle of a busy street or in the back seat of the car. I prayed and prayed, and when nothing changed, I waited. I waited for the fear to pass, or for God to relieve my anxiety. *I remain confident of this: I will see the goodness of the Lord in the land of the living.* I tried to meditate on this passage from Psalm 27. But I wasn't in the land of the living. I was in some dark twilight between worlds.

When I prayed for relief, I sometimes prayed in tongues. I'd been taught by my friends in Tribe that to pray in tongues—that eerie, mesmerizing practice—was to speak directly to God without the Devil interfering. It's believed that the Devil doesn't understand tongues, only God does, so when one is in a particularly fraught or troubling situation or needs to make a difficult decision or is on the verge of postpartum collapse—tongues.

Praying in tongues wasn't something readily discussed, but everyone I knew who belonged to a church where tongues were part of the culture, the belief system, recognized it when it happened. It was unmistakable. Tongues are believed to be a manifestation of the Holy Spirit, one of the gifts left behind after Jesus ascended to the heavens, a story told in the second chapter of the book of Acts in the New Testament. Sometimes the speaker prays in a language unknown to them, or sometimes it's a kind of made-up language known to no one at all. To those who practice it, tongues is the mark of a true believer.

I began praying in tongues myself a few months after joining Tribe in New York. Sabrina had told me to pray for the ability, to ask God for it. I did, and not long after a mysterious language tumbled from my mouth, words that sounded like nonsense, or an invented patois. Sometimes it sounded vaguely Arabic or Hebrew, at least to my ear. The *ch ch* rising from the back of my throat, the *eee* and *ooo* swirling between hard, guttural *d* and *g*. It felt a bit like the first full drop on a rollercoaster or the second after your feet leave the diving board. A thrill through my body, exhilarating and strange. At the time, I pushed away any thoughts of doubt, thoughts about how bizarre and almost scary the ability was, like possession. Or worse, that it could be the very nonspiritual collision of my intense desire to fit in and the power of suggestion. Instead, I accepted it as part of my life as a Christian, and after a while, I didn't think much of it, even as I regularly practiced it. I prayed in tongues with my postpartum prayer group, and eventually someone in that prayer group recommended a Christian therapist who prescribed medication for me. *Tongues led me to a doctor who'd led me to medicine that healed me*, I thought. I'd been *obedient*. I gained back some faith in that experience, faith I feared I'd lost when my prayers for relief seemed to have gone unanswered.

Tongues was not part of the tradition at Holy Immanuel, however. The first couple we met and got to know there had also come from a religious background where tongues was practiced. "They don't do that here," the woman told me over latkes and gefilte fish at a church-sponsored Seder dinner led by a Messianic Jewish Rabbi. She'd heard me murmuring under my breath during one of the opening prayers and recognized what I was doing. "It's frowned upon," she said, screwing up her nose and smiling sympathetically. "Put it away if you want to fit in." I was slightly taken aback, but grateful for the warning. I'd later learn that like most mainline denominations, the Christians at Holy Immanuel found tongues and other remnants of charismatic or Pentecostal

Christianity, what Tribe had been most closely aligned with, to be odd, embarrassing, a little creepy, maybe. I took the woman's advice and hid this part of my practice.

But now in Budapest, as when I was deep in postpartum depression, it seems to me that tongues is an important part of my spiritual toolkit, one I've been taught to use in situations when nothing else works.

As I listen from the kitchen for the male voices in the other room and lay out slices of bread and cold cuts, I release a flurry of clicks and coos, rolling my tongue against my teeth, speaking the strange language quietly enough not to be heard but loud enough to feel that familiar rush. This way I can participate in the conversation without participating in it. Since leaving New York, I've become accustomed to this dance of small compromises that makes translating my faith—from north to south, and across denominational lines—possible. Making sandwiches while praying in tongues in Central Europe is yet another one.

What also returns is the sense that every moment is unscripted, the sense I developed in the early days of Tribe, when anything seemed possible, when it felt like the world was thick with God's presence. Even though things are not quite as I'd hoped, I'm filled with the belief that we are here for good and important reasons. I pile the sandwiches on a clean plate and, with a stack of napkins in the other hand, walk back into the living room to serve them.

It doesn't take long to realize that despite my attempt to escape it in Houston, there is darkness in Budapest too. I imagine the depths of the Danube, the river that divides the city, still littered with the bones of Jews who were shot on its banks during World War II, and with the remains of Hungarian rebels who dared try to overthrow a brutal Communist dictatorship. As we cross the river each morning in our borrowed car, Matt reminds me and Sydney, who is strapped into her car seat in the back, that the Danube snakes through ten countries and more than a dozen cities—Vienna, Novi Sad, Budapest, and Belgrade among them—before finally reaching the Black Sea. At night, we watch the lights on the bridge named for a long-dead Hungarian princess sparkle like diamond bracelets on a blue velvet sleeve. Budapest is darkness and light. A captivating memorial to beauty, art, and terror. There is a feeling of heaviness everywhere we go, and it isn't the jet lag or culture shock. The city seems to sag beneath its weight. Like my expectations of motherhood, my naive expectations of what it means to be a missionary in a European city with a complicated history are quickly breaking down.

"Don't forget," the missionary says as we gather in Erzsébet tér—Elizabeth Square—a few weeks later, "this may be someone's only chance to hear the Gospel." The lush park has a gleaming white marble fountain at its center and is surrounded by pubs and coffee bars, halal shops and pizza restaurants. The missionary continues, "You never know when God will call a person home."

Home, we understand, is a euphemism for heaven, and we nod. The missionary has on another version of his uniform, shorts he would've worn to mow the lawn back in Houston and a collared golf shirt. Matt fiddles with the cable connecting his acoustic guitar to the portable sound system. The generator whirs, emitting a faint smell of gasoline. I stand beside the microphone and try not to make eye contact with the well-dressed Europeans sipping beers and flirting. They lounge in the cigarette-stubbled grass just beyond where we're setting up. I feel a pang of homesickness for New York. I remember naps in Washington Square Park after an all-night rave, my head heavy with the Ecstasy I'd taken the night before. I look over at Matt. He's focused on the cables, tuning his guitar. He's not making eye contact with the young Europeans either.

"Who's going to be willing to give their testimony today?" the missionary asks our group.

I have a version of my testimony, the story of how Jesus came into my life and saved me, that satisfies this requirement. When I do share it, I find that young women respond to the way I frame it, the way we're taught to frame it, as a narrative of rescue and redemption. It isn't just a religious narrative, after all, but a literary one—one we are raised on, embedded in almost every fairy tale. The knight in shining armor is another version of the Jesus story, and it resonates. The women I talk to on the streets of Budapest are curious about Matt and me, about our story. Though I don't exactly portray Matt as a knight, I suggest that God has ordained and blessed our relationship, that our faith has gotten us through hard times. They want to know if God will do the same for them. They want to know if God will bring love into their lives, if God can make that love last.

"How about you do it, Jimmy?" the missionary suggests. "We'd love to hear your story."

Jimmy stands at the back of our small group, and we all turn to face him. He crosses his arms and walks over to the makeshift stage.

"Awesome," I say.

"Do it, man," Matt says with a reassuring smile.

When Jimmy approaches the microphone, I notice a few young women who were sitting in the grass make their way closer, to a park bench. The girls are thin and pale in an off-duty-fashion-model kind of way. One has almost translucent blond hair and a large tattoo of an eagle on her forearm. They are visibly interested in Jimmy—athletic, tanned, and

Texan—if not in his religion. As they extract themselves from the patch of grass, balancing handbags and cell phones, cans of beer and cigarettes, I notice they've left a clutch of young men behind. The young men, some of whom are napping near the fountain, are tattooed and dreadlocked and are dirtier, rougher around the edges, than the lithe Hungarian teenagers sunbathing beside them. The tourists with expensive cameras and backpacks march determinately around them through the grass, careful not to step on an unfurled hand, or wayward foot, or an empty beer bottle.

"I know your story will be powerful," the missionary says to Jimmy. The girls, now seated on the cobblestones at Jimmy's feet, smile up at him.

I exhale and look at Matt. I'm relieved I won't have to give my testimony, not today.

Matt leans toward me. "I still can't believe this place." My eyes dart to the elegant buildings, to the Hungarians strolling the grand boulevard or clasping hands over tiny coffees. I envy them despite myself. Matt does too; he's come alive in Budapest. He reaches for my hand. "Let's never leave," he says.

"You guys ready?" the missionary asks as he approaches the microphone to introduce Jimmy.

In our meeting at the ministry center earlier in the day, we discussed logistics—who would pick up the equipment and who would set it up—but we also prayed for signs that God would move powerfully, that through our efforts he would bring the harvest of souls to himself, the souls of unbelievers. We'll be looking for signs, for coincidences that lead us to specific people: a young woman with a weariness about her, a young man sitting on the periphery of his group of friends. People who are vulnerable, in other words. We call these meetings with strangers *divine appointments*.

While Jimmy is speaking, Matt and I walk over to a young man who has been watching us since we set up the equipment. He's been perched on a park bench, separate from the nappers. As we approach him, I pray in tongues, letting the torrent of syllables tumble from my mouth for just a few seconds, asking God to open an opportunity, to create a connection. By now, this young man has been in the park for several hours, listening quietly to the music and to Jimmy's message.

The sun sinks, bathing the trees in soft pink light. The young man carries a worn red backpack and wears expensive hiking boots. His name is Mark, he tells us. He's from California and is on a mission of his own, to see his father's home country. Mark's father was a Hungarian soldier during the 1950s, when Moscow was cracking down on those Soviet satellite countries, like Hungary, drifting precariously toward democracy. Mark tells us that his father was one of the organizers of the failed 1956 revolution, a student-led uprising against the Soviets. While Mark's father's co-revolutionaries were being rounded up and shot, or imprisoned in secret torture chambers, he sneaked out of the city on the back of a truck, never to return.

"My father won't talk about Hungary," Mark says, as we sit on the park bench in the growing dusk. "That's why I came. I want to see it for myself."

"It's not what I thought it would be," he continues, smiling. "What about you guys?" He motions to the guitars and drums and microphones.

"Me neither," I want to say, but don't. Instead we explain to Mark about the ministry center, about our church in Houston and the concerts we've been giving every day.

"Are you here to convert people?" Mark asks.

"It's more about sharing—" I stutter, "what we've learned.

The good stuff. Just sharing life." I want to kick myself for my hesitation. It's awkward to talk about this, no matter how fervently I believe it. *The Lord sent us to share the gospel with the unsaved.* I can't bring myself to say those words aloud, even though I know it's why we're here. Maybe being asked to make sandwiches has shaken me. I'm less confident than I should be, and it shows. Mark and Matt talk until Jimmy finishes his testimony.

The missionary motions for us to help him break down the equipment.

"Need help?" Mark asks.

"Sure, man," Matt answers, looking to me for confirmation. "That'd be great."

Back in California Mark played drums in a band, so he and Matt talk about ride cymbals and drumheads while they break down the kit and pack the myriad parts away into the plastic cases we brought. While they're working, Mark confesses that he doesn't have anywhere to stay for the night and is planning to camp in one of the city parks.

"I'm not sure they'll let you do that," I say. "The Rendőrség love to fine Americans. You can set up your tent in our backyard if you want. Or you can stay in our extra bedroom."

I look at Matt. There's room for Mark in the mansion; we're not using three of its five bedrooms. Yet my offer hangs in the air as Mark looks to Matt and then to me again. We've known him for forty-five minutes. I think of what my mother would say to us opening our doors to a strange man, with not just our safety but our daughter's safety to consider.

"Yeah, why not," Matt says, "we have room."

"God gave us this massive house," I say, temporarily recovering myself. "A free gift to us, one we're happy to extend to you." When we arrived, we attributed the luxurious house to God's grace, but lately, it's proving to be more than we bargained for, harder to maintain than we expected. Still, I believe the house is a sign, even if it's a complicated one. It's confirmation that we're in the right place at the right time. We believe meeting Mark is also a kind of sign, exactly the sort of divine appointment we're hoping for. Matt, Mark, and I carry the equipment to the van, and then help unload when we arrive back at the ministry center. After saying our goodbyes to Jimmy and the rest of our team, the three of us hop on a crosstown bus for home.

Mark doesn't pitch a tent in our backyard, of course, but stays in one of the spare bedrooms, and not for one night, but for a month. He proves helpful around the house. It takes hours to sweep and mop, and Mark always offers to pitch in, usually before Matt does. Since coming to Budapest, I've learned that missionary life is stridently gendered, and most of the missionary families who live here year-round are more traditional than we are. The wives stay in their borrowed Hungarian homes with their often-large numbers of children, while their husbands are out preaching and proselytizing. The wives negotiate the half-empty grocery stores, prepare homeschooling lessons, cook and clean, while their husbands draw maps of regions with the most unsaved people, teach Bible studies, and plan outreaches. The wives view housework and child-rearing as their mission. While I value their work, it's not what I've come to Budapest to do. Matt and I share the responsibilities—of playing music, giving our testimonies, and meeting Hungarians—equally. Before we arrived, it seemed that this arrangement could work, but it's becoming much harder to pull off than we expected. We're often exhausted and hungry, and our clothes are dirty. "*We* need a missionary wife," I joke to Matt, and we both laugh, though we don't really talk about it seriously. I can't help but wonder if Matt wishes I was different, we were different.

I also feel this tension in the way the male missionaries—not just the one we came to work with but others—interact with me. They ask me how I'm liking motherhood and they ask about Sydney, who is at home with a Hungarian teenage babysitter while we are at the outreaches. Sydney toddles bravely over the mansion's cold marble floors and is picking up Hungarian words and phrases faster than we are.

In Budapest, I try being a ministry leader *and* a wife and mother, but I struggle. I can't make it to every staff meeting, though it's part of my job description. The laundry piles up as usual, and we order in pizza—curiously served with corn baked into the cheese—several times a week. I feel I'm being judged in this regard, as though the suspicion I had after Sydney was born, that *mother* and *wife* are synonymous with *good* and *Christian*, has proven true.

Mark helps with the groceries, makes beds, and does the dishes. He's handy at the borrowed mansion, but he's also happy to help out around the ministry center—painting and repairing the old building. He seems to have a talent for these things. He also tags along to all our outreaches, helps load the gear into the van, then unpacks it and sets it up. We don't talk about the religious purpose behind what we're doing; instead we focus on the logistics. We know Mark hears the testimonies and the preaching, but we don't know how he feels about them, and as the summer drags on we feel increasing pressure to confront him. Will he be saved? Will he choose Christ? These questions wiggle into my consciousness every time he and I talk. Mark has told us that his parents are nominally Catholic, the de facto religion of most Hungarians. Also like most Hungarians, Mark and his family are nonpracticing, he says. His spiritual interests are similar to what mine were before Tribe. He's drawn to new age-y spirituality, soft-core mysticism, yoga, astrology. Nothing too organized or specific.

As the days stretch into weeks, the uncertainty that began for me with the sandwiches has bloomed into restlessness. Though I say I believe that without Jesus the leggy Hungarians twined on the grass will go to hell, I envy their freedom. At night, as we head home from a day of preaching in the park, when my feet are aching and I should be eager to see Sydney, to be home with my small family, I instead want to stop at a café and throw back shot after shot of sweet, peppery pálinka—the locally made apricot brandy. I want to dance in the clubs and eat in the restaurants. At home on a rare day off, when I should be praying or reading my Bible, I put on my old green bikini and lay a towel on the tiled patio. I stretch my body in the sun, and as I do, I watch Mark watching me—just glances as he moves through the house, acknowledgment of my presence, nothing more. But I relish it. I want to be seen, and maybe not just as a religious person but as a woman, still young and strong. I don't know how to be both, though. Not in the life that I've chosen. I note a growing awareness of my body's hunger, its insistence after so many years of a life in which Spirit has taken precedence. I don't want Mark, not really. But I want something. I begin to worry that my hunger cannot be satisfied by God.

I also begin to worry that it isn't the Hungarians who need us, but we who need them. We need to feel like there is some purpose to the religion we've chosen, to the hours and dollars we've spent uprooting our lives and the lives of our children to bring a message to a country that seems to be doing just fine without it.

Regardless of my doubt, I want Mark to pray to *accept Jesus as his Lord and Savior*, and I want to be able to report back to the donors at Holy Immanuel that he did. This is the proof the church needs and wants, that sending us was the right decision. Maybe it's the proof that I need. Everything about Mark shows evidence of the Spirit, I think: kindness, patience, generosity. We shouldn't have to say or do anything; God will bring the threads together for him. But it seems as though Mark is content to carry on mopping, sweeping, painting, and hanging out with us without a confession of faith.

"So where is Mark with the Lord?" the missionary asks. I turn away so he doesn't see me roll my eyes. We're packing up for another outreach at Elizabeth Square, and Mark is busy outside, loading gear into the ministry center's minivan.

"He's not into organized religion," I stammer. "But he's really open. I'm waiting for the right moment to talk to him about it." I pick up a microphone stand to bring to the van and pray in tongues again, a murmuring swell under my breath. I ask God for a sign, a window, a bolt of lightning, anything. I've never led anyone in the prayer of salvation before—the goal of most missionaries with potential converts—and it feels like an essential initiation.

When we get to the park, a group of young men are playing a game of Hacky Sack on the spot where we usually set up the stage, so we set up our instruments and speakers beside them. I recognize them from the day we met Mark; they napped while Jimmy gave his testimony. They're visibly put off by our intrusion, though soon after we strike the chords of the opening song, they quit their game and seem to tune in to what we're singing, and, later, what we're saying as another testimony is offered at the microphone.

As we wind down the outreach, storm clouds gather over Elizabeth Square, and big drops of rain begin to fall. The sun is blotted out so quickly that it appears as though night's fallen, though it's not yet three o'clock. Matt, Mark, Jimmy, and I rush around, dragging equipment under a concrete overhang, trying to protect it from the sudden weather. The Hacky-Sacking young men rush under the same overhang, and we find ourselves shoulder to shoulder.

"We like your music, man," one of them says to Matt in

a heavy Polish accent. "We're on the festival circuit this summer. Following a few bands, camping out, you know, going from city to city." They tell us about their adventures, and we offer a few stories from our time in Budapest.

"You know, if it was just the music, it would be okay," one of them volunteers. "But when you guys, Americans, come here to Europe and get on the microphone to talk about your religion—it sucks, man."

I look at Matt. Maybe this response is exactly what we'd not been ready to hear when we'd avoided eye contact earlier in the summer.

"It's like you're speaking another tongue, another language. You don't know what life is like here in Europe, but you get up there on a microphone and you speak as though you do know. You take up this space." He extends his arm toward the rest of the park, now swamped in the deluge, "as if your American religion is one size for all. It's not, man. We don't speak that language."

I can see on Matt's face that the young man's words are landing with him. No one has ever said this to us before, pointed out what might be obvious to onlookers, what I haven't allowed myself to admit until this moment—that we have no business here. Everything we're doing here is arrogant, tone-deaf—our American version of Christianity, with its folk-rock music and emotionally manipulative testimonies. Though the young man's words are landing with me too, I look at Mark and wonder how this conversation will impact his decision about Jesus. We've grown so close to him. But are we close to something that matters?

"Are we going to make it?" Matt asks half-sarcastically after the young Poles trudge toward the boulevard, motioning to the equipment, maybe trying to shake off the conversation, to lighten the mood. I'm standing beside Mark, both of us looking weakly at the still-pouring sky. Water swirls in tiny eddies, inches from the speakers and cables.

"Man," Jimmy says, "it's gonna flood."

Lightning streaks the sky, above the old buildings on Káldy Gyula Street, and I see my opportunity.

"I'd feel much better about this storm if I knew we were all going to the same—place," I say. I can't bring myself to finish the thought. The same place *when we die*. Even though I'm still absorbing an awareness that our entire presence here is suspect, I won't shake my sense of purpose.

"What do I need to do?" Mark asks, as if he too has been awaiting this moment. The young Polish men round a far corner, and as they disappear, so does my hesitation, at least for the moment.

"Pray with me? I'll give you the words and you can just repeat them." A chill creeps up my back. I scramble to remember the words of the Sinner's Prayer, the prayer of salvation, because I know this window is a narrow one. When the sun returns, the spell will be broken, the opportunity missed.

"Okay," Mark says. "I'm ready."

"Just repeat after me," I say. "Jesus…"

"Jesus," Mark says.

"I'm sorry for all the things I've done that have led me away from you."

"I'm sorry for all the things I've done…"

"I repent, and I ask for your forgiveness," I say.

"I repent and ask for forgiveness."

I think of the moment with Sabrina in the bar at the Soho Grand. How confidently she offered the words and how eager I was to repeat them. I look for some sign on Mark's face, some emotion to tell me that he believes what he's saying, that these words matter.

"Lord, I invite you to come into my heart, and I ask you

to help me live my life for you." I haven't forgotten the words after all. Almost as soon as we both say *amen*, the chill spreads to my hands and shoulders, climbs like a virus to the top of my head. Mark looks the same as he had before— except maybe relieved.

A few days later, Mark packs up his red backpack and his unused tent. He's already stayed longer than he'd planned to, but his departure feels abrupt. He hugs us goodbye in front of the ministry center, promises to keep in touch, and makes his way to Keleti station for a train to Prague, where he'll continue his backpacking trip.

When we get back to Houston, I send Mark a message on Facebook. He's living with his girlfriend, and I can see from the pictures that she's pregnant. "Are you living out your new faith?" I write. "Have you found a church? How can we pray for you?" My questions are as much for me as they are for him.

I tell our supporters from Holy Immanuel the story of the young American man whose life we "impacted," whose "faith journey" we influenced. I never get a reply from Mark. But every time I tell his story, it's the young Pole who returns to me. He's soaked by the sudden storm, bouncing on the soles of his feet like a prophet. With his image comes the dawning awareness that my faith will have to change if it's going to survive. That in order to speak about God, about anything, I have to start by listening.

Withdrawal

"Do you think about him when you masturbate?" the therapist asks breezily.

I shift lower on the velour couch. I cross and recross my legs, stunned. Have we ever talked about masturbation? Is masturbation something adults assume all other adults do?

I've just told her about the man I think I might love. The man I'd met at the arts conference I returned from a few days ago. The intense attraction, the texts.

"Yes?" I answer tentatively.

This man and I were part of a cohort of writers and artists who were holed up on an island off the coast of New

Hampshire for two weeks of classes, workshops, and lectures. I'd been a writer all my life, but since becoming a Christian I'd limited my writing to worship songs and devotional-themed blogs. After Budapest, I was looking more closely at my own discomfort with the church, not as a sign that I was a failure as a Christian but with the tacit acknowledgment that maybe being a Christian—or at least my idea of what that meant— was failing me. Taking part in this arts conference was a way, I thought, to try to write my way through that discomfort.

Matt and I were also in a difficult place. We were back to passing each other in the hallway, not speaking much, not connecting. He'd lost another job. But after meeting the man at the conference, the man was all I thought about. That preoccupation anesthetized me, all my other concerns numbed out.

I'd sought out this therapist because I was worried about all these things.

"If you think about him when you masturbate, you may be a sex and love addict," she says.

"A what?" We've been working together only a few months, but I've been more honest with her than I have with anyone, therapist or otherwise, in a very long time. I'm worried she's misunderstood me, something I said. I take a deep breath and wait for her to say more. I listen to the trickling of the small electric waterfall on the coffee table. The walls are painted white and decorated with framed landscapes—another waterfall, a snow-capped mountain range.

"Sex and love addictions are really common," she says, and takes a sip from a glass of water. "Frankly, many people will fit the profile at some point in their lives."

I'm disoriented by her pronouncement—that the "addict" designation, assigned to almost everyone I've ever loved, could apply to me too. I'm sure I'm not an addict. Matt's the addict. He never touches alcohol now. Matt's addiction has a locus. It can be seen, felt, found in space and time. How can my distraction, my preoccupation with this man—someone I hardly know—be an addiction?

On the fourth night of the conference, I snuck into the main hall, a dull, damp, carpeted room on the ground floor of the center. There was an upright piano I'd been staring at for a few days, hoping for time alone with it, to play and sing. The event had been more grueling, emotionally and spiritually, than I'd expected. In the past, moments alone at the piano were also moments alone with God. They revived me, helped me focus, but that night it wasn't God I wanted to sing to. I wanted to feel the physicality of singing, the breath in my body, the vibration in my throat. This, more and more, had become my focus. A different kind of prayer, maybe.

After a few minutes at the piano, I noticed him in one of the stiff chairs, sketching in a leather-bound notebook. I recognized him; we'd been introduced a few days earlier. He was a visual artist, recently engaged. Lean and muscular, with a wardrobe of threadbare flannels, flecks of gray at his temples. I glanced up from the piano for a moment, but he didn't meet my eyes. He continued drawing, and I started the next song. Soon, I forgot he was there. I forgot I was there. When I looked up a second time, he was gone.

The next day he knocked on the door of my hotel room. "For you," he said, and handed me a rusted railroad spike. He said he'd found it in the seaweed and driftwood on the beach a few blocks away. It looked like it had been in the water for a hundred years. I held it in my hands, cold and heavy and dangerous. I was unsure what to say. He seemed nervous and said something about being true to one's self, a reference to the song I'd been singing the night before. "Thank you?" I said, but he'd already turned to go, walking down the hall to the stairwell.

I didn't know what to make of his gift. I placed it on the dresser and tried not to think about its implied violence, how incongruous it was with how he appeared in my doorway when he gave it to me, sweet and nervous, sheepish almost. Later, I went into the art studio when he wasn't there. He was working on a large canvas, an abstract with layers of blue and gray, so dark it looked almost solid black. It was intense, and beautiful. But there was nothing in it to help me puzzle out the spike, and I soon forgot about it, caught up in the swirl of the conference. We didn't say much else to each other over the days that followed, but we locked eyes more frequently than we should have, over the coffeepots in the morning, during the evening lecture. His gaze, when I held it, was frighteningly steady. I was always the one to look away first.

On the last night we stood close, talking, at a crowded party. It was the first time we'd spoken at any length since he'd showed up outside my door. A buzz of flirtation and gossip filled the overheated room. We were all tired, ready to go home, but squeezing out the last few hours before returning to our real lives.

"I had an affair with a married woman once," he said. "It didn't end well." I took a sip of my beer. "I was in love with her, and her husband wanted to kill me. It was bad. Really bad." He shook his head and looked at his feet.

I was wearing a concert T-shirt with the neck cut out and ripped black jeans. I felt strong and pretty and a little drunk. Outside the lights along the shoreline flickered against the blue-black sky, the air damp and cold. By then, the women I'd spent most of my time with during the conference—the married women—had all gone to bed. The only single one among us had secreted off to some other single person's room.

His eyes were glassy and fixed on a point above my head. He pulled out his phone to show me a picture of the married woman he'd been in love with. She looked like me.

"What about us?" I said abruptly, trying to regain his attention. "About this."

He looked up from his phone and palmed the front of his black collared shirt. A saint medal hung on a silver chain around his neck. I brought the beer bottle to my lips again. I could feel the party start to tick down. The door from the conference room to the street swung open as people went to their rooms or left to smoke, and the music got softer. I had an early flight. It was late, and I was running out of time.

"Maybe it'll be enough for you to know that I want you," he said finally. "Maybe that will be enough."

I flushed. I had his attention now. My want was enormous, like a sinkhole. For years I'd filled it with God, but that space was now vacant.

"Walk me home," I said as he backed up, maybe contemplating an escape or another beer. "Walk me home and we'll talk about it."

My hotel room was off-site, a few blocks away. Outside, I hooked my arm into his.

"We have a decision to make," he said. Wind whipped up from the water and tangled my hair. We knew we'd be seeing each other again; we'd both committed to return for the next conference in the summer, but a few months seemed like a decade.

We stopped in front of my hotel. He was taller than any man I could remember standing this close to. I thought of my empty room, my clothes thrown on the bed, the three outfits I tried on before I left for the party. I pressed my face against his shirt. No smell of soap or sweat or cologne, nothing but the night, its clean blue smell. The wind kicked up again, and the vacancy that was once God announced itself. *I'm a mother, a wife, a minister.* I stepped back and let him go, left him standing in the circle of yellow streetlight.

I had just relayed all this to my therapist when she asked me the question about masturbation.

"Sex addiction is a spiritual disease," she says. "The addict replaces God with a person. A lover, or a potential lover. I think you should go to a meeting, Cameron. Soon. Maybe today."

I find a women-only Sex and Love Addicts Anonymous group that meets near my house at an old church, and I go that night, eager to collect enough information from the meeting to prove that I'm not what my therapist thinks I am. While listening to the stories of others in the circle, I spend the entirety of my first meeting reminding myself of all the ways I'm nothing like them. A week later I return and spend my second meeting acknowledging all the ways that I'm just like them. I return again and again, week after week. I don't tell Matt. I say something vague about going to group therapy when I slip out every Monday evening at quarter to seven. He nods, generally uninterested as long as I've left dinner for Sydney. When I'm at home I'm keeping secrets—about the man, about my spiritual doubt—but at the meetings I don't have to. The veil of anonymity, though I don't trust it completely, gives me just enough of a sense that it's safe to be honest there. I begin to look forward to the meetings for this reason.

I listen closely at SLAA, especially to the stories that circle back to difficult childhoods, to eating disorders and sexual assault, to physical and emotional abuse. Though the women who attend that Monday night meeting come from different backgrounds with different religions and careers—some are doctors, or lawyers, some are PhD students, or sex workers—our stories, especially our childhood stories, all sound eerily familiar. When I feel like I've gotten the hang of meeting etiquette (*no cross talk; keep it brief; focus on the solution, not the problem*), I share my own story.

As a kid, I didn't know why my parents' relationship was so volatile. I learned that later, when I was fourteen and their divorce was in process. They were still living together because neither could pay rent on a separate apartment while still carrying the mortgage on our home that proved difficult to sell. As the financial pressure mounted, my father repeatedly accused my mother of cheating on him. She and my younger brother had been the usual victims of my father's paranoid accusations. I'd managed to stay out of his way for the most part, to be obedient and invisible enough to avoid becoming a target. One day, I told him I didn't need a ride to my weekly voice lesson. I tried to sound casual about it. I didn't want to be alone with him in the car, didn't want to give him an opportunity to grill me about my mother or say something biting or hurtful as he would sometimes do during those short car trips. Instead of accepting my request, or even ignoring it, he stood at the bottom of the staircase, holding his car keys, and told me I was a whore just like my mother. I only knew what *whore* meant because I was deep into reading *Flowers in the Attic* by V. C. Andrews. I'd come across the word and looked it up in the *Merriam-Webster* dictionary my father kept on his bookshelf.

I didn't know how this word could apply to me, but I did understand that by branding me with it, he transferred his open contempt for my mother to me. I felt ashamed, though I couldn't understand why. I knew I wasn't a whore. I was a virgin, and the dictionary made it clear that one cannot be both. It wormed its way into my idea of myself anyway. Throughout my adulthood, I would spend a lot of religious energy trying very hard not to feel the shame of this thing my father had called me.

I think of all this as I attend weekly SLAA meetings over five months. As I listen to the stories, I notice how the framework is similar to that of the testimonies I've heard, and given, on the streets of Budapest. Only in the SLAA stories, it's not God who rescues us from our broken childhoods and bad decisions but *the program*. I recognize something else that's familiar: the profound comfort that a structured worldview—with identifiable solutions to our problems—can provide. I'm wary of yet another system that requires belief in order to belong. I've entered into this program as I'm questioning Christianity, and I learn fairly quickly that in order to participate fully in recovery, I will have to believe in God. It doesn't have to be anything other than "God as I understand God," but I will have to recreate a notion of God to work with, and even that idea feels exhausting.

SLAA offers a stay against chaos, however, and I am in chaos. Since that night at the conference, I've texted constantly with the man. We've spoken on the phone and talked about our next meeting. After a week or so of messages about books and art and the feelings between us, he told me we couldn't talk at all. "We have responsibilities," he wrote. "We need to get back to them." We'd be seeing each other again at the end of the summer, he reminded me, at the next arts conference, but his sudden unavailability plunged me into a weepy, dark mood that lasted weeks. Almost as soon as I recovered myself, he'd text or email again. I'd feel buoyant, elated. After a few days, the guilt, the fear of getting caught, would become too much. I'd put an end to it. Or he would. Then he would reach out again, and the cycle would continue—grief, elation, grief. I was consumed by it. It was interfering with my ability to concentrate, to care for myself or my daughter, to lead worship.

At the SLAA meetings, I hear the difference between an

addiction to alcohol and an addiction to sex and love described as the difference between a substance addiction and a process or behavioral addiction. An addiction to sex and love falls into the latter category. It's not the thing itself that brings reward but the private rituals built around it: the eye contact, the texting, the emails, the *talking*. I see myself in this—it's the beginning of the process (getting out the phone, composing a text, checking social media) that triggers the chemical wash, the light-headedness. Though it hardly seems worthy of being called an addiction.

"I've had *intrigue* at work this week," someone will say at a meeting. She'll describe a flurry of increasingly intimate email exchanges with a colleague, or locking eyes with a man or woman across a room at a party and feeling an instant thrill. In the past I would have called this *attraction*, but even I can see that the obsessiveness that follows is what makes it different. "I walked past his (or her) desk ten (or twenty, or thirty) times, hoping to catch a glimpse," or "I drove past his house," or "I can't stop checking my phone." Half a dozen women nod their heads as they listen. It reminds me of what I'd learned about myself when Sabrina put me on the "man fast" back in New York—that I spent a tremendous amount of time and energy on these kinds of interactions. "That person you're locking eyes with is probably the only other sex and love addict in the room," one of the old-timers will say, a member with more than a decade of sobriety. I learn that addicts can *intrigue* (verb) with someone they're not even sexually attracted to—meeting for coffee, texting, having long, deep conversations with a boss or coworker or a friend's spouse. The high comes from the danger of the interaction, its inappropriateness. The more unavailable the object of affection, the stronger the pull, and the better the payoff. There is a line that shouldn't be crossed between two reasonable people who are romantically unavailable to each other, a line most people agree on. The compulsion to play at the edges of that line, to test the boundaries—this is what others I meet in the meetings are doing. It's what I'm doing.

I'm still not entirely sure that I'm a sex and love addict, but learning these things gives me a sense of control, a sense that I'm taking steps. It helps me to see why I've always wanted what I couldn't or shouldn't have—whether a man or a religion. It helps me to understand something Goethe said about the color blue: I was and would always be drawn to not what met me but what drew me after itself.

I have a hard time connecting with other women in those meeting rooms, perhaps because I'm reticent to admit that I'm an addict. Or because as soon as the meeting ends, after we've held hands in a circle and chanted the serenity prayer in unison, I look down and bolt to my car. I'm heeding the warning that a different therapist had given me years ago— he said to never attend twelve-step recovery meetings because I could be recognized. I often was recognized, in fact, at a coffee shop, or restaurant—"Aren't you the worship leader at [fill in the church]?" That recognition could threaten my job, threaten my standing in the community as a "Christian leader." Though I haven't made many connections yet, it's clear that friendships between women in SLAA are a big part of what keeps them in it.

When I meet Fi, she's sitting on a squeaky chair at the far end of the room, holding a cup of weak coffee. Her spiky blond hair is pushed back from her face by a workout headband. I'm running late, as I often am. The woman leading, a redhead in a nurse's uniform, is reading the preamble from a laminated piece of paper. *Sex and Love Addicts Anonymous is a Twelve Step, Twelve Tradition oriented fellowship based on the model pioneered* by Alcoholics Anonymous. *The only qualification for SLAA membership is a desire to stop living out a pattern of sex and love addiction.* Fi's eyes are closed, her hands shoved into the pockets of a down vest. She wears exercise leggings and a hooded sweatshirt. *To counter the destructive consequences of sex and love addiction, we draw on five major resources: 1. Sobriety—Our willingness to stop acting out in our own personal bottom-line addictive behavior on a daily basis.* As the meeting leader continues to read, Fi rocks gently in her seat, eyes closed, nodding her head as if amen-ing in church.

Fi's Irish accent reminds me of Sabrina's English accent, how the comforting melody of her speech often softened its content. When Fi had been most active in her addiction, she explains, she was living in Dublin and working in the film and television industry. I listen to her describe her own romantic disasters with humor and candor. She talks about her willingness to reinvent herself, to switch religions, geographic locations, or even careers for a partner. I see myself in her stories.

I think about the changes I underwent while Matt and I were dating—how I became a Christian, stopped pursuing secular music, moved to Houston, and traded a career as a publicist for one as a music minister. I'd done all the things Fi described. At the time, I thought those changes had nothing to do with Matt or my desire to be with him. I thought it was what God wanted from me. If being with Matt is what God wanted, I should be willing to do whatever it took to make that happen. I start to see that I conflated wanting to be with Matt and wanting to please God.

After Fi finishes, I raise my hand. The meeting leader nods at me and smiles, granting me permission to speak next. A month ago, I returned from the second arts conference where I again saw the man I think I might love. "I went to his room," I blurt. "He asked me to. I stayed almost until the sun came up. It was—intimate, but we didn't sleep together. I want to—" Fi's eyes are closed and she's nodding again, maybe encouraging me to continue. "I don't know how to stop wanting to." I see a few other women nod their heads. I want to say more, but I don't know if talking about it that way, reliving it out loud as I'm doing in my head, is going to help me, or anyone.

I decide to stick around after the meeting rather than escape to the parking lot. I walk toward a group of women by the stack of folding chairs, with Fi at their center. I'm still thinking about what I've just confessed to a room full of strangers. "Has anyone ever told you that you resemble an Irish actress?" she asks me, smiling. "I can't remember her name, but she's very well known in Ireland." Fi squints at the ceiling as if to find the woman's name there. Yes, I tell her, someone had once told me that, with the same Irish accent. Years ago, in New York, I'd managed to befriend the sister of a famous actress, who then invited me to the Gramercy Park apartment they shared, where I met a famous Irish film director. After listening to my demo CD, a collection of the first songs I'd ever written, he made the pronouncement.

"I used to work for that director," Fi says matter-of-factly, a shine to her blue eyes despite the fluorescent lighting. "It's the same actress I'm thinking of." She pulls out her phone to search for a photograph. A thrill runs through me. Not only because I'm flattered by the comparison but also because of the sense of a shared experience, a recognition. In college, before Christianity, I'd have called this *synchronicity*, the Jungian term for this kind of uncanny coincidence. In my more religious days I would've called it a *God moment*, a sign from the heavens to let me know I'm heading in the right direction, like the divine appointments we were looking for in Budapest.

I smile at Fi, and our conversation eventually spills into the hallway and then the church courtyard. Fi has been with her partner for fifteen years. She's been faithful, she says—the meetings keep her faithful. Belief in something or someone she hesitates to name, a *higher power*, helps too. I haven't yet heard from someone who is in SLAA and actively trying to preserve a relationship. Many of the women who share their stories are in the process of leaving or being left, in the midst of emotional chaos, like I am. Fi and I have a shared sense of the stakes should the program, or our commitment to it, fail. When she invoked the famous film director, she spoke to me from my past, a past that felt like it had belonged to someone else, to a version of myself that existed before Christianity changed everything about me, when I'd been pursuing other kinds of dreams for my life and for my music.

When I pull out of the parking lot that night, I notice that the SUV parked beside me has my initials, CDH, in its license plate. Though I've just had the experience with Fi, I'm hesitant to see this as a *sign*, as one of those *God moments*, as I might have in the not-so-distant past. "Just a coincidence," I say aloud. I flick on my headlights and pull out onto the busy street. As I drive, I wonder if at least part of what draws me to recovery are religious ideas about sex and love. The reservation of sex for marriage, that any sexual contact or even interest outside of marriage is a sin, are certainly ideas that I've absorbed from Christianity. The notion that what I'm doing, romantically fixating on a man who is not my husband, is aberrant and needs to be corrected—is that also a Christian idea?

I don't know if my marriage will survive, but I want to be able to say that I tried, that I worked on my side of the problem—that I was willing to get help. Going to meetings allows me to believe that I'm doing that. Maybe this will be part of the case I make to whomever I'll need to make one to—Matt, my family, Matt's family—if we file for divorce, if it comes to that. My participation in SLAA is calculated in this way. Being good, doing good, following the rules, any rules—this is probably the thing I've been most consistently addicted to in my life, truth be told. If I follow the rules of SLAA—or even if I just appear to—I get approving nods from the women I'm slowly getting to know. I get pats on the back from them and from Fi, and it makes me feel good. I come to crave that affirmation, as I did from Sabrina and Tribe.

Even though I know this, and though I'm also conscious of the parallels between Christianity and SLAA, I keep going back. I don't want to see meeting Fi and my initials on that license plate as *signs*. I know that license plates run chronologically—it just happens to be the year that CDH is being used by the Texas Department of Motor Vehicles. But in spite of myself, it confirms my instincts. Maybe there's something in SLAA I need. *It works if you work it.* I should submit to the program even if I don't agree with every aspect of it. Even if I'm not yet a true believer in twelve-step recovery. I've faked belief before.

There is a key difference between SLAA and Christianity. To be a good Christian, at least in the circles I've frequented, means to hide the transgressive parts of myself. To bury my hunger and restlessness under piety, reverence. I was honest in that meeting room about what I've done, and what I want to do. And I wasn't rejected for it. For now, it's a great relief just to be somewhere I don't have to lie.

Submit

It's a hot late-summer morning, and Matt and I pack up his car for the drive to Austin to sing at an author's sold-out book launch event. We met the author at St. Mark's, a small Episcopal church on Houston's south side. I was hired about a year ago to lead a stripped-down, jazzy service on Sunday evenings there. I'm still at the Refuge on Saturday nights and Sunday mornings, and I make the twenty-five-mile drive to St. Mark's every Sunday afternoon. It makes for a long weekend, but being there, in the beautiful old chapel with vaulted ceilings and stained glass, feels like an actual refuge. And meeting the author, who writes books on healing and being in the world, seems significant. It feels good to be around serious writers as I begin taking my own writing more seriously.

I'm relieved by the timing too. It's a rare opportunity—I haven't sung outside churches in more than a decade, and preparing for the event, learning new songs, and rehearsing will give me something else to focus on, at least temporarily. The author doesn't offer prescriptively Christian views in her work, and the music she's asked me to sing isn't Christian music, but rather a collection of songs she mentions in her books: the Beatles' "Let it Be" and David Gray's "My Oh My." Yet I worry that if she knew that I'd been unfaithful to my husband, she wouldn't want me anywhere near her event. Fidelity and stability in marriage have been a require-ment in every church job I've ever had, and though this is not a church job, I still have a hard time overcoming my shame. The author and I met at a church, after all, and the church is the basis for my perspective. For now, I do my best to hide my worry. I keep working hard to appear as though everything between Matt and me is fine. I use the veneer I've learned from the many Southern Christian women I've known through the years. *We're doing great. Bless your heart for asking!* The public face so different from the private one.

Because St. Mark's isn't like the Refuge, isn't like any evangelical church or community that I've been a part of, I can't help but wonder if there may be more grace for me here. More room for me to be human. What if I could actu-ally go to the priest here and confess, as so many Christians do? Like most Episcopal churches, St. Mark's is not aligned with the social and theologically conservative platform that is the hallmark of evangelicalism.

But it's not just the aura of progressivism that draws me to St. Mark's. It's the sacraments: small, everyday rituals enacted with quiet reverence. *Most merciful God, we confess that we have sinned against you in thought, word, and deed. By what we have done and by what we have left undone.* These words from the confession of sins resonate. What I have done is clear to me. What I have left undone, and the cost of leaving it undone, is more complicated.

Once we're on the freeway to Austin, Matt drinking his coffee and driving too fast, I assume my usual role of DJ and navigator. I select another Patty Griffin album, our go-to for these drives. I check the map for upcoming rest stops and calculate how long it will take us to get to the venue—a 2,500-seat indoor amphitheater just north of Texas's capital city. I fidget with my water bottle and check my phone. Before we left for Austin, I told Fi that maybe I should tell Matt what happened. A day alone together seems like a window of opportunity. I'm not sure that I'm prepared for his reaction, though. Whatever it might be—I can't stand continuing to hide this from him.

"There's so much about me you don't know," I say as we fly west on Interstate 10, past a Holiday Inn, several car dealerships, a Starbucks.

"Like what?" Matt asks.

Heat rises off the asphalt. Pickups and horse trailers begin to crowd out the hatchbacks and luxury SUVs as we get farther away from the city. Restaurants and hotels thin out to reveal open fields browning. We pass tumbleweeds, the shiny coats of grazing cows, the occasional Czech-themed gas station that sells kolaches—pillows of dough injected with fruit compote—and framed needlepoints of the Alamo. I change the music.

"What is it I don't know about you?" Matt asks again.

"I have an entire inner life I don't share."

Since my beliefs about God, about us, have been changing,

I've shared fewer of them with Matt. How else could this preoccupation with another man have formed so powerfully? It needed a vacuum within which to grow.

"Share it with me," Matt says.

I glance at him behind the steering wheel. His honey-colored beard is flecked with gray. "I can't," I say. I wish I could tell Matt about my inner life. I wish I could tell him anything. But I lose my nerve.

Later, somewhere around Bastrop, between taco stands and BBQ joints, I say, surprising us both, "I think we should separate."

He doesn't turn his head; he keeps his eyes on the road. I look at him. He adjusts his grip on the steering wheel.

"I'd have to get an apartment," he says, finally.

This is not the first time I've brought up separation. I did once before, and it had nothing to do with another man. It had to do with the gulf between us since Budapest, with the miscarriage I'd suffered a few years later, with Matt losing his job at Holy Immanuel and then Faithbrook. It had to do with years of mostly unvoiced frustration.

"I couldn't continue to play in your band on Sunday mornings," he says. "You know that, right?"

I begin to imagine leading the all-male band on the big stage at the Refuge by myself. How difficult it would be to articulate key changes and tempo adjustments without Matt there to translate for me. Since I gave up playing piano in front of an audience years ago, mostly because Matt believed getting out from behind the piano would free me up as a vocalist, it meant that I didn't have an instrument to articulate what I wanted, musically. I relied on Matt and his acoustic guitar. It's hard enough to get male musicians to take me seriously with Matt around. Without him, would it be possible? Deep down, I have no doubt that I could do it—could handle it, technically—but I have so much muscle memory built up through this dance of deflection between Matt and me that I've forgotten myself, what I'm capable of.

"What about Syd?" Matt says.

In the past when I brought up separation, Matt flatly refused to consider it. This time he's listening. I inhale. I haven't thought this part through, not really. Matt is devoted to Sydney. They're devoted to each other. He's gentle with her, present. He is, I sometimes think, closer to her than I am, especially lately. He always manages to find ways to enjoy being with her, where I've experienced the moment-to-moment pressures of mothering a baby and then a toddler, and now a kid, as relentless. I feel as though to enjoy her, to take my eye off the ball of constantly protecting her, of making sure she's healthy and safe, is a kind of betrayal of my responsibilities. Matt somehow manages to be both her friend—someone who takes her to baseball games and movies and out for pizza—and a good father. I envy their easy closeness.

Sydney has been growing more and more anxious as things between Matt and me deteriorate. She calls for one of us if we're out of her line of vision for more than a few minutes. If we're in the house and one of us goes outside or upstairs while she's playing a game or drawing—"Mommy!" she yells, until I come running. She's vigilant, like I am in many ways, and I'm anxious that she's developing anxiety. After years of happily sleeping over at her grandparents' house or at friends' houses, she's afraid to go to bed at night without one of us next to her. She insists that I recite a particular prayer in a particular way in order for her to fall asleep. Maybe her anxieties about sleep mirror mine. It's when the house is quiet, when Matt is asleep beside me and Syd is asleep in her bed, that I spend hours down internet rabbit holes. I'll type the man I think I might love's name into a search engine and follow the breadcrumbs. Sometimes I'll find his art, an article he's written, or an abandoned blog. Sometimes his comments are about his religious beliefs; he wonders if those beliefs are legitimate. It will be late, two or three, before I shut down the computer or turn off my phone. Maybe Syd senses that when I'm putting her to bed I'm already a million miles away.

Though Matt and I are unhappy, I can't imagine him willingly separating from Sydney. I can't imagine telling her that Daddy isn't going to live with us anymore.

"Let's give it a year," I say. I pull this time frame randomly, but I go with it. "What if we work really hard, what if I go to therapy, and you go, and we go to meetings, support groups?"

Matt glances at me. Dry, flat, central Texas rolls by.

"A year?" he asks.

"A year," I say.

The venue tonight is set on a craggy limestone hill surrounded by stands of Spanish oak, cedar, and cypress. Inside, I set my bag down in the greenroom, stocked with snacks and drinks, and follow Matt to the stage. A sleek, black concert grand piano glints in the low backstage lighting. I look at the rows of seats and imagine the thousands of people who will fill this hall in the next few hours. I stand beside the spot marked X with electrical tape, in front of the microphone as I have so many times before, and wait for sound check to begin.

Matt's friend David, a musician and producer who lives in Austin, has joined us to play piano tonight. Together we wheel the massive grand out of the wings and onto center stage. Matt and David rib each other, and Matt and I act as though nothing has happened, as though we've not just been discussing the dissolution of our more-than-a-decade-long marriage. Our familiar rhythm: concealing what's going on between us by stepping into the current of a performance. David cracks an inside joke about musical gear, or sound technicians, like the one who is brooding behind the soundboard right now. It's mildly antagonistic, and I notice the sound guy's increasing huffiness. This is typical, almost predictable, and I'm reminded that I'm musically dependent on Matt. Guitar in hand, he is the musical director, the one who communicates with the surly sound technicians and rehearses the band. He makes sure everything runs smoothly. I'm released from that pressure, so I can "just sing." When Matt and I play music in church together, or anywhere, I always take a back seat, even though I've been putting bands together and directing them since college. The musicians and techs we work with are almost always men, and Matt strikes an easy rapport with them. *Wives, submit yourselves to your own husbands as you do to the Lord* reads Paul's letter to the Ephesians. On nights like this, I get a glimpse into the seamlessness of my world, how I tote my evangelical ideas—about women, about power, and about marriage—into spaces where they aren't necessary.

In our church rehearsals over the years, my struggle to "submit" was painful. I never directly addressed a problem or question I had. Instead, if one of the musicians repeatedly played the 1 chord instead of the 4, the C instead of the F, I'd say to Matt, "Babe, don't you think something sounded off in that last chorus?"—even though I knew it hadn't merely sounded off; it had been off. I believed that to keep the peace, for the music to be the best it could be, I had to tamp myself down. Play dumb, just a little. It was excruciating, and confusing for everyone else because it was clear that I was uncomfortable. By submitting, not just in music, but in our marriage, I robbed us of my full participation in both. It would be years before I understood that our flip-flopping between churches, our relative inertia in terms of producing new music, and our romantic stalemate all stemmed, at least in part, from the watered-down version of myself I was offering.

On a stage in this neutral environment, I'm about to perform for the largest crowd I've stood in front of before. The author doesn't ascribe to the belief that I should submit to my husband, and she certainly has no expectation that my husband should lead this band. My musical abilities have landed this gig, nothing else. But I don't remember how to perform, at least when Matt is involved, any other way. I wait for Matt and David to tune up their instruments, to calm down the sound guy, and to begin the sound check.

By the time the house lights are dimmed, the stage lights come up, and Matt strums the opening chords of Leonard Cohen's "Hallelujah," that current we stepped into earlier is strong enough to carry us, to wash away the tension. The amphitheater rings with our voices, his tenor and my alto and the metallic twang of his Gibson acoustic, bound tightly in a resonant braid. It's always like this: the music we make is beautiful, no matter what else is going on between us.

After the event, Matt and I drive downtown to a high-rise hotel and check in for the night. Despite the late hour, there is the smell of cedar and grilling meat, the crunch of gravel underfoot. Austin reminds me of our first years together. When we visited in the past, Austin brought us back to our beginning. This time, though, Austin feels like a museum of a former life. The old landmarks are hard to recognize—in the city and between us too.

I draw the curtains and undress in front of the television. The room is cold, and I scuttle into the big white bed. Matt lies down beside me and props up on his elbow. He moves to kiss me, but I turn my head. He runs his hand over my breasts and stomach, slips his fingers beneath the band of my panties. I lift my hips and he moves his mouth down my body. I pull him up by his beard.

"Let me make you feel something," he says. "Let me." I usually don't let Matt go down on me. It makes me feel too naked, exposed. My own desire folded down into a complicated origami. I let him this time, let him move from my neck to my belly to the part of me that aches. The part of me I've kept, in some ways, from him. If I can surrender myself to Matt like this, maybe I can still love him. Be *in love* with him. He drags his mouth across the slope of my hipbone, sending a current to my pelvis, my spine, the top of my skull. I let him stay there for a long, long time. While the air conditioner drones. While the TV flickers in the dark room. While I fight with my mind and try to stay present with him. With us.

Look Too Closely

I would've attended Koinonia, where we'd worked before the Refuge, even if I wasn't employed there. The young, socially conscious congregation worshipped in a converted warehouse just a few miles south of downtown Houston. The dark-haired pastor was semifamous for being at the forefront of a loose, nationwide collective of churches known for their focus on social justice, advocacy for the disadvantaged, and a strong critique of the materialism of American life. *Koinonia*—in Greek, the sacrament of bread and wine—was offered in every service. It was a trend among these emerging Christians to adopt practices, like weekly communion, more reminiscent of Catholicism than of the Southern Baptist Convention, the denomination that spawned most of them. They disguised their affiliation with the SBC, one of the most socially and theologically conservative denominations in the country, but they never fully broke from its financial support or influence. They liked the liturgical calendar and obscure, difficult-to-pronounce Greek or Hebrew names for their churches, names that worked hard to distance them from their roots. They liked religious art and candles and iconography. They liked Radiohead and exposed brick and tattoos (preferably of Greek words like *koinonia*). They liked espresso, C. S. Lewis, and CNN.

They also liked money. Specifically, the pastor at Koinonia liked to spend the money that came in through tithes and offerings on his pet projects—the bookstore, the coffee shop, international travel—not on salaries for staff members. He chronically underpaid his staff, and Matt and I were no exceptions. In fact, after he hired us, I heard he'd boasted in a recent staff meeting that part of his leadership strategy was to hire "unqualified" people in order to save the money he would've spent on more experienced employees. Matt and I were not unqualified; we had years of experience, and our previous combined salaries had set us up for a modest, but comfortable, life. In our first meeting with the pastor about the job, he admitted that he knew the salary he could offer us was far less than what we'd need to make ends meet. "We'll find the rest," he enthusiastically promised. "We'll go to the congregation and ask for it directly." We could raise financial support, he said, like we told him we had done as missionaries to Budapest. "You'll be a key part of *our* mission." He said he'd send us to South America, or to Africa to work on their mosquito-net project. We might even be able to accompany him on an annual trip, a *pilgrimage*, he called it, to Israel.

Though it seemed odd to us to have to "raise" our salary in order to work for a prosperous church, we trusted him; we saw him as our spiritual leader, our *pastor*. He was so different from the baby boomer pastors we'd worked for before. He was our age and seemed to share our values, and he'd already written several popular Christian books by then, books we'd read and relished. He was smart and charming, and everyone we knew in ministry wanted to work for Koinonia. Perhaps the challenge would teach us to trust God. God wouldn't let us take a thirty-thousand-dollar pay cut without finding some way to provide.

The music at Koinonia proved a good distraction from our mounting financial woes. It was very different from the soft folk music we were encouraged to play in other churches— poor imitations of Cat Stevens and James Taylor, holdovers from the touchy-feely Jesus movement of the 1970s. The songs we played at Koinonia were driven by loud drums, electric guitars, and earnest, keening vocals. Every church service was like a rock concert, urgent and raw. It wasn't the kind of concert that the people at the Refuge thought they were evoking with their smoke-and-lights show—it was like something you stumbled across in a divey hole-in-the-wall, the kind of musical experience that could change your life—that had changed my life, first as a teenager and then as a young songwriter in New York. *And the heavens will open wide*, I'd sing on the plywood stage built into the back corner of the warehouse, the room dark but for two wrought-iron candelabra and a few stage lights. The guitars blazed behind me, and hundreds of people in the congregation sang along. I felt, while I was singing, that such a thing was possible, that the heavens could open, that it was all real. Later, Matt told me that the musical freedom we were given (the pastor didn't check our set list to make sure the songs were theologically accurate, or that they fit neatly with the theme of his sermon) and the experience of so much passion and focus from the congregation was unlike anything he'd ever experienced in a church.

But as time went on, it became clear that money wasn't the only problem. Hidden beneath the environmentalism and social justice were Koinonia's Southern Baptist, hyperconservative ideas about sexuality, gender roles, and church leadership. On the outside, Koinonia was a liberal, socially progressive church. On the inside, it felt sexist and homophobic. While I worked there women weren't offered leadership roles, not outside of children's ministry. I watched the church's male leaders steer female volunteers and staff members toward childcare and away from preaching, toward food preparation and away from teaching scripture. Though Koinonia invited women to occasionally speak on Sunday mornings, it was only ever friends of the pastor, women with best-selling Christian books they were on tour to support, for sale in the church's bookstore. Their *speaking* was distinguished from *preaching*, a religious loophole that allowed women in complementarian churches to give readings or presentations without threatening male leadership. I also watched church leaders limit the participation of the church's LGBTQ members—they could bake the communion bread, for example, and their financial gifts were welcomed, but they couldn't be married in the church. I'd later learn that their children were refused baptism—a particularly cruel policy of exclusion—and though Koinonia tried to keep it quiet, I'd also heard that they fired a female minister after she came out. These policies weren't included in the church's "What We Believe" section on their website. Only experience at Koinonia over several years made it clear to me. Because I believed in the church's overall mission, and in the pastor, I told myself he was playing a long game, that he was working to change the system from the inside out. Also, I wasn't yet willing to give up how important, vital even, it made me feel to work there.

Meanwhile, Matt and I were falling deeper into debt, putting groceries and doctor's visits and our car payment on a credit card.

After months of trying to schedule a one-on-one meeting with the pastor to talk about his promise to help us raise the rest of our salary, he agreed.

"I'm going to ordain you," he said. We were sitting across the desk from him in his cramped office on the second floor of the church, above the coffee shop. The sound of the espresso machine whirred below.

"Both of us?" I asked. I was giddy.

"Yes," he said. "Ordination will help with your taxes." Matt and I were both silent. "You'll be able to write off your housing. That should help." He looked down at his desk and shuffled the papers there. Gone was the enthusiasm from our initial meetings. He seemed vaguely annoyed. Even though I knew that changing the way we did our taxes was not going to help in the way we needed it to, at least it was something. I fantasized briefly that ordaining me was about more than money, that it was the first step in changing the culture at Koinonia, of inviting me, and other women, into real leadership. Next, I could become an elder or preach. I imagined he would share his decision to ordain me on social media. It would cause an uproar among the more conservative evangelicals at the church and in the wider church community. We could figure out the money later, I thought, if it meant being a part of this landmark shift.

A few weeks later, I got a signed and dated certificate naming me an ordained pastor at Koinonia, which I framed.

I waited for an invitation to preach or to become an elder, but those never came. By then, we'd made close friendships at the church, had sung at the baptisms and weddings and funerals of people we'd grown close to there. Its members were our community, and we called them our *church family*. I spent birthdays and anniversaries and regular Tuesday nights in their homes, and they in ours. I chose to wait. I chose to believe that even if I couldn't change the culture, other women would soon.

Not long after we received our ordination certificates, Matt was offered a better-paying job at another church, and took it. I stayed at Koinonia, hopeful that the pastor would offer me a job that would legitimize the work I continued to do weekend after weekend, that would give me a seat at the table and a salary to match my experience and commitment. Then one afternoon, during a rehearsal with a pianist I'd invited to play with me for an upcoming Sunday service, I learned that the pastor had offered *him* my job the night before.

"We were at dinner and he asked me," my friend giggled conspiratorially, like a teenager who'd just been asked to prom. I felt the blood drain out of my face. Dinner? It had taken me months to get the pastor to return an email or a phone call. I was told he was busy, out of the country, unavailable.

"He offered you which job?"

"Worship pastor," my friend said. Worship pastor was the job I had been doing, but without the official title. I had no official title.

"You mean my job?" I asked, stuttering.

"I assumed—you—didn't want it," he said.

"I want it," I said.

"But you'll stay and sing, right? We definitely want you to sing."

During the long, awkward conversation that followed, I learned that my friend had not only been offered my job, but at a much higher pay rate. I hadn't wanted to believe that being a woman had anything to do with the pastor's refusal to acknowledge me professionally, but after my friend's announcement, I couldn't *not* believe it. In the end, I would never do the thing that Saint Paul forbid women from doing in that passage from Timothy—I would never "teach men" at Koinonia in the way that I'd hoped. Maybe in part because I believed, and had expressed openly more than once, that I *was* teaching men, that I was preaching every time I opened my mouth to sing. My female body was an issue, would always be an issue. I saw it clearly for the first, but definitely not the last, time.

I accepted the job singing at the Refuge not long after. Matt and I were trying to dig ourselves out from under the mountain of debt we'd acquired working for Koinonia, and the Refuge's offer was one I couldn't afford to turn down. This happens often with music ministers, and with pastors too. The church that can afford to hire you is not necessarily the church in which you would choose to worship. Ministers often refer to a job offer as a *call*, a request or directive from God. Implicit in the notion is that some sort of sacrifice will have to be made in order to be obedient to God, to accept. Maybe it's a sacrifice of comfort with the church's politics, maybe it means moving to an unfamiliar neighborhood or city. Though we humans may not understand it, we're supposed to trust that God knows what God's doing. Because the feeling of being thrust into a new congregation is an expected and unavoidable part of life in ministry, ministers often explain it with the language they have for everything—spiritual language.

For more prominent male pastors, *call* and *financial benefit* often become intertwined. Though ministry is not supposed to be about getting rich, many pastors in big suburban mega-churches—including several at the Refuge—are doing just that. It's not hard to say "God called us here" when "here" means full health benefits and paid sabbaticals, when it means your kid gets to go to the church-run private school for free.

At first, the offer from the Refuge seemed like a godsend. The salary and benefits and relaxed schedule meant that I could exhale. I could spend more time on my writing. But soon it became clear that the over-the-top smoke-and-light shows were the least of the challenges I would face.

Throughout my career as a worship leader, which by then spanned eleven years, I was often met with blank stares and sweaty palms from men I worked with. The sexism wasn't just overt, like the instruction to make sandwiches in Budapest, directing all questions to Matt, or avoiding one-on-one meetings with me or driving in a car with me alone—common practices among evangelical men. It was also evident in more subtle behaviors, like talking over me in meetings or never looking me in the eye. I don't know whether these men were aware of their own religiously sanctioned misogyny or simply acting on tradition—though those two impulses are really no different. Most evangelical men I worked with were reassured by Matt's presence, and it allowed me to ignore the misogyny that was in the church, and not only in the church but in me. Misogyny I'd internalized. The joy I got from singing made this delicate emotional and theological dance, these denials, worth it. I loved to watch the congregation move from distraction to reverence over the course of a single song. From where I stood on the stage, I watched their crossed arms open and drop like petals. Sometimes I watched body after body surrender, their eyes tilted to the ceiling, to God or to the Holy Spirit, whatever they believed was up there. I was looking more closely at the benefits than at the painful things that made those benefits possible. As long as Matt was with me, I was shielded from it, in a way.

The job at the Refuge was offered only to me, which has forced me to face my lack of recognition as a minister, as a leader in my own right, not just a "singer." It has finally begun to cost me—dignity, integrity, salary. These ideas about men and women aren't foundational for me; they're ideas I've learned since my baptism. I'm finding them harder and harder to swallow as the fervor of my conversion gives way to a kind of spiritual midlife, a battle of competing desires.

It's been just over five months since the eighteen-year-old girl's funeral, and about as long since I started attending SLAA meetings regularly. It's also been five months since I told Matt we should give our marriage a try for one more year. I climb into his truck for the long drive from our townhouse near downtown Houston to Greenhills, to the Refuge. Sometimes it seems our whole relationship takes place inside a car. It's Sunday morning, so we've already done the Saturday night service. Today we'll repeat it twice, at nine and eleven, exactly as last night, including every prayer, every announcement, every seemingly improvised quip or lighthearted on-mic joke. An older pastor has taken over preaching duties this weekend because it's Commitment Sunday, the day in the year when the congregation makes financial pledges in support of the church's million-dollar operating budget. It's an important fundraising weekend, and the church doesn't want to take any chances leaving it to someone less experienced. The older pastor has worked at the Refuge for decades, since before it was a megachurch. He's well liked and known for his tendency to become emotional during his sermons. His anti-LGBTQ politics are less well known among the congregation and staff, and they're as yet entirely unknown to me. He often makes off-color jokes in the greenroom before services. He talks about sex and sexuality almost all the time. I smile at him politely but avoid being alone with him, and assume the other female staff do the same. It's just after seven, and the Houston landscape quietly flies past—sturdy magnolias and oaks crowd the roadside, washed in white morning light. We pass the El Crucero Sport Bar with its hand-painted sign and mangy pit bull pacing the parking lot. Climbing vines cover telephone poles and abandoned houses, and wind-stripped cypress trees sway in the sunny January chill. As Matt drives, I picture the man I think I might love. It's last summer, late at night, and we're standing inches apart. He's asking me to stay. My back is against the door of his room, one of my hands on the doorknob. A pickup truck rumbles on my right. Matt turns the car radio to NPR. I don't mind these long drives to the Refuge with Matt, even if they are mostly spent in silence.

I put earbuds in and hit play on a song by Lykke Li, a Swedish singer I often listen to on drives like this one. Her voice warbles and cracks, but it, and she, seems to ache with a rawness I understand. My own voice is raw because I'm battling a perennial and somewhat extreme reaction to pollen from the blooming oak trees, which causes me to lose my voice, at least partially, every winter. As I listen to Li, I envy the way she can use the imperfections in her voice to articulate something true about the pain of bad, even destructive, love, the kind of pain I'm in now. I only ever sing about God, and I have yet to find a way to make my pollen-ravaged voice work in the same way. I'm paid to present unwavering belief through the songs I choose and the way I sing them. No doctor or allergist seems to be able to understand my voice loss, why it's so resistant to treatment, and I'm not yet looking for the metaphor.

Matt pulls the truck onto the 610 loop and heads for the toll road that will take us to the Refuge. The tire shops and cheap hotels give way to acres of cleared land. As I glance into the lane beside me, I notice the license plate of the SUV one car length ahead has my initials. I'm looking for signs again, like the patterns in weather, that lightning bolt I was waiting for in Budapest, the summer storm during my baptism.

Lykke Li sings "I Know Places" into my ear. What if there was somewhere the man and I could go? I've recently applied to attend another conference, one that's held at a university within driving distance of where he lives. I imagine that he'll somehow find out I'm there, will hear it from a mutual friend or see an announcement I've posted online. I imagine that one afternoon while I'm at the conference, he'll drive down from his seaside town.

Or maybe by the time I get to the conference, I'll be cured.

The women in SLAA meetings talk about music and how it can strain one's commitment to *no contact* with a *qualifier*, the person who qualifies one for this program, like an addiction to alcohol might qualify one for AA. Some music makes it harder to keep the vows we've made to ourselves, makes it harder to stay away. As we drive, I think about how the Christian music I've written is also designed to affect vows, in this case the vows the congregation makes to God. I think of how, when I was losing my own ache for God, the music brought me back to it.

At the Refuge, I use music to inspire the congregation not only to make vows to God but to commit their time and money in the way the church wants. Though I try not to focus on money, this particular January weekend, when the older pastor will ask the congregation to *pledge*, they will write the amount of their annual contribution on tiny squares of cardstock. Though it seems to me a crazy way to run a business—not on actual income, but on promises—it works.

When people inevitably don't keep their promises, and the amount of money pledged doesn't match the amount given, a small number of wealthy donors, sometimes just one, are called upon. That donor's influence, in terms of deciding what the church supports and what it doesn't, cannot be underestimated. Unlike in politics, there is no limit to how much an individual can give, and historically every penny of that gift is tax deductible. The biggest donors have the biggest influence, and in Greenhills, as in Houston—cities built on the oil business—the wealthiest donors tend to be conservative white men.

While the church would not exist without monetary commitments from the congregation, I hope that when they sing with me today, their bodies open and relaxed, they'll also be making vows to some larger mystery. The mystery won't visit or bring a casserole when someone dies or loses their job or has a crisis of faith, I know. It's the woman from the bake sale, the blood drive, or Mommy's Morning Out who will fulfill those needs, and those programs rely on financial support. The style of the Refuge is not mine, but I want to believe there's room for something real here. Maybe it's not for me to determine how a person interacts with God, the style of presentation, or which aspects of church life are worth supporting. What I do determine is the music.

More and more often, however, it's the pastors who choose the songs they think will highlight and amplify a specific emotion, move the congregation to action. The pastors are under pressure to get commitments and to raise that one million dollars. The more people pledge, the more secure the budget is, and thus all of our jobs, but the kind of emotional manipulation favored at this megachurch makes me squirm. I suspect the younger pastor, the one with whom I helped lead the teenager's funeral, the one with the tattoos and

ponytail, thinks it's as unlovely as I do. We've shared a secret
eye roll now and again. Like me, he needs his job. He keeps
his opinions to himself.

We park just outside the Refuge, and I slide the keycard
I've managed to remember today into the electronic reader.
I push open the heavy, reinforced door that lets us into the
backstage area.

The older pastor is sitting in one of the artisan-made metal
chairs in the greenroom, recently ordered from an expensive online catalogue. I remember the last time I sang during
a service when he preached. Afterward he hugged me too
hard and too close, an aggressive embrace that smashed my
breasts against his chest. At least in my experience, Christian
men, especially pastors, never hug like that. They practice
what I sometimes call, a bit cynically, the Christian side hug,
which offers a reliable framework for what could otherwise
be a problematic interaction. Because sexual ethics are a
primary evangelical obsession, simple greetings between men
and women are loaded with protocol. At the time, the hug
bothered me, but I let it go. It hadn't happened again.

"Hi!" I say too brightly. "How's it going?" I lay down my
backpack, walk to the electric kettle, and dig a bag of Throat
Coat out of the drawer marked "tea."

"Good. Glad you're with us this weekend, looking forward
to it," he says with a slight Texas accent.

Matt claims one of the armchairs, and I sit cross-legged on
the low-slung tweed couch. As the band files in, Matt starts
to tune his acoustic guitar. I make jokes with the band until
the countdown clock pops up on the high-definition fifty-
four-inch LED monitor on the wall. It will begin counting
down five minutes before the service, enough time to take
our places on stage before the house lights come up. We'll
wear special in-ear monitors that wirelessly connect us to the

sound guy, the service director, and each other. Still an hour before the service, the small black pocket monitors sit piled on the reclaimed wood coffee table. We'll eat a catered meal together (with a gluten-free, dairy-free, grain-free option), go over logistics (has the volunteer doing the announcements sound checked her mic?), and discuss cues ("I'll start the prayer with something like, 'Friends, the Lord has called us to give to his work on earth,' and that will be your cue to start playing the guitar softly underneath me—"). Then we'll hold hands and pray, disperse to the couches and expensive chairs to make small talk, finish our meals, and wait for the service to begin.

"How much weight are you bench-pressing now, John?" the older pastor asks of the guitar player between bites of taco salad. He raises an eyebrow and reaches toward John, sitting beside him, to poke his bicep. He half-mockingly flexes his own thin arm and grins.

The man who held my job before me was a bodybuilder—the band referred to him and his wife as "fitness models"—and his interest in diet and exercise sparked a band obsession, which has continued long after the church hired me. His departure had been poorly handled by the church, and the all-male band was rightfully displeased. I wasn't pleased with it either; I'd felt awful for the band, and I've mostly made a tentative peace since then, though I take the almost constant talk of carb-cycling and bench-pressing as a subtle rejection of my authority. I haven't been inside a gym in three years. I have nothing to say when they start talking about diet and exercise, and they know it. The men in my band have never worked directly for a woman minister before. They've backed women singers, but have not been led by a woman. Acceptance of me is slow to come, even two years into my time here.

On Christmas Eve, I came backstage after singing "Silent

Night," hoping for a moment of meaningful reflection with them, maybe a chance to acknowledge a difficult though mostly smooth year of working together. I found them sprawled out on the carpeted floor, side by side, comparing push-up form and bicep size, a pastime they're now repeating with the pastor.

Just last night an unarmed black man was killed by police. Now our phones begin dinging with news alerts. The Refuge is an almost exclusively white church in an almost exclusively white, conservative Republican suburb. I immediately brace myself for racist comments and Fox News–driven propaganda.

The pastor begins a story from his time in seminary in the seventies. Racial tension was high, he explains, but he and his wife chose to live in a predominantly black neighborhood to work on reconciliation.

I look to Matt, who has set down his guitar and is now watching the pastor.

As a Texan, he continues, he was surprised to encounter racism in the liberal northeast. "We thought we could bring the kids together—the white kids and the black kids—but when we had the black kids over to our apartment, to work on homework or have supper with us, we'd inevitably come outside in the freezing weather to find our car had been vandalized."

His eyes glisten as he tells us how important it was for him to build connections with the kids in the neighborhood. "We kept on, of course, kept inviting the kids and they kept coming."

I force myself to look down at my phone. This story in which he casts himself as a white savior doesn't surprise me, but I don't call him out on it. I imagine the silence that will fall over the room if I do speak up, the looks I'll get. In a few years I'll learn to ignore those looks, to turn awkward silences—especially around divisive issues—into productive conversations, or at least try to. But today I'm still trying to get along here, to minimize my judgment. I tell myself to respect the pastor's authority. To keep quiet and stay in my lane.

There are about twenty of us: the band, the sound engineers, the technical director, hospitality volunteers. "Gracious heavenly father," the pastor begins, "thank you for the faithfulness of your servants. Send us out to do your will and your work today, by the power of the Holy Spirit!" The countdown clock shows five minutes until the service begins. A glossy clip-art image of a forest—a photo probably taken somewhere in the Pacific Northwest—shimmers behind it. 1:34...1:33...1:32... "Amen," the pastor says. "Amen," we repeat.

I grab my in-ear monitors and head out onto the stage. I warmed up vocally, something I never do, while the band ate in the greenroom, because I'm desperate to get my voice back to full strength. I press my cold hands against my neck as I make my way to the spot in front of the microphone, where the video cameras can get a clear shot of my face. A second countdown video begins on the two large screens that flank the stage. Vapor pours from the smoke machine behind the drum kit, filling the stage and obscuring the first few rows of seats. I can make out the shapes of bodies in the folding chairs, black silhouettes against the purple-blue lighting. I can't see anyone's eyes. I hear the sound engineer's voice in my in-ear monitor. 5...4...3...2...1.

I'm shivering again, like I did during the girl's funeral, and I reluctantly pull my hands off my neck. A spotlight comes up slowly and Matt strums the opening chords to the first song, one the pastor chose. I open my eyes and focus on the red exit sign at the back of the room. I begin the lyrics. My voice is raspier than I'd like, and I don't have nearly the control I'm used to, especially on very high and very low notes, but it holds. Then as I sing the next line, about a wave crashing over me, my voice cracks as if on cue. It's something I would normally be horrified by, a slip of air sailing out through the note and into some register almost too high to be heard by human ears. It's a rare moment of honesty.

When the service is over, the band starts breaking down their gear, packing up instruments, and lowering amps off the stage. Daylight slices through the dark room every time someone opens the internal door between the Refuge and the rest of the building. It's noon on Sunday, and I've survived the weekend. As I begin to make my way to the backstage area and then to the greenroom, a woman walks up to the foot of the stage and motions for me.

"Thank you," she says between sniffles. "I lost my grandmother last weekend. Your song—" she reaches into her purse for a tissue. "Just thank you," she says again, waving it in front of her face.

I hop down from the stage to hug her. I don't know her, and she doesn't know me, but it doesn't matter. This is why I do this, I think. When the woman leaves, sending another shock of light into the room, I head backstage to collect my purse with a slight bounce in my step. Matt is already in the car, waiting. Despite my rough voice, despite it all, I feel good; someone was moved by what I did here today.

I'm walking along the elevated walkway directly behind the stage. The "backstage area" is really just a delivery bay, a sort of oversized garage housing set decorations for the various seasons: A dozen fake Christmas trees and boxes of lights. A table saw. Dozens of coiled cables. Fake flowers and raffia for Easter. A pulley system for a lighting trellis. Extra chairs and tables. I see the older pastor walking toward me; he must've forgotten something on the stage. His sermon this weekend—despite the impassioned call for increased financial giving—was good, at least what I'd heard of it. I'd spent most of the sermon scrolling through my phone in the greenroom.

I raise my right hand in a high five, elbow lifted, palm above my shoulder. When the pastor is about ten feet away from me and I'm holding my hand above my head in this way, I say, "Great job this weekend!" and mean it. I'm proud of the work we've done. When he's about a foot away from me, he lowers his hand instead of meeting mine in the high five and drags it, lightly and quickly, from the bottom of my armpit to the top of my ribs, over the outside of my left breast. I say nothing. Stunned, I keep walking toward the greenroom, where I spend five minutes looking for my purse, exactly where I'd left it.

Outside, in the car, Matt is scrolling through his phone, staring at the unremarkable suburban landscape, his fingers drumming cartoonishly on the steering wheel. He's waiting while I walk off the stage, through the backstage area, and into the greenroom. I know this—point A to B to C—but what happened in between?

By virtue of *the divine made flesh*, Christianity takes special issue with the human body. Jesus Christ becomes human flesh and suffers human pain as a result of being in a vulnerable human body. Greedy pilgrims run fingers over plaster recasts, imagine grabbing the hem of Christ's garment like the bleeding woman in the Gospels did. But where does one religious body end and another begin? Whose hand has the right to touch the stigmata, the brow, the wounded side of Christ? *Everyone's does* is the answer.

I used to think that the people who were drawn to the church—pastors, worship leaders, even members of the congregation—were better than other people. That they were people who wanted to be better, to do better. They were trying, at least. As I cross the church parking lot, I think that maybe I was wrong and the opposite is true. There's no God in this moment to talk to; there's no impulse in me to mutter a prayer or speak in tongues under my breath as I once would've.

"You good?" Matt asks as I climb into the passenger seat. I look back at the Refuge, worried that the pastor will come out, will get into his luxury sedan parked a few cars down from us.

"No," I answer. "I'm not. I'm not good at all."

"What's wrong?" Matt asks.

I start to cry.

"I don't know. Nothing. Can we please get out of here?" I slink down in my seat, willing Matt to pull out into the road. I want the truck to disappear in the sea of cars heading for the freeway. I want to disappear.

"What happened?" His volume is escalating, but he does as I ask and drives.

I hold my breath until I know we're clear of the Refuge. I wipe my nose and eyes with the back of my hand.

"I'm okay, I think. Something happened. I think something happened." I don't have language for this. I hear myself say, "Maybe it was an accident." I'm already absolving him.

"I'm pulling over," Matt says.

"Don't. I'll tell you. Just drive, please," I say. "He—touched me. My breast. I don't know if it was an accident," I repeat, "or, no. I know it wasn't accident. I feel sort of sick."

"Who touched your breast?" Matt demands.

"The pastor," I say.

"Are you fucking serious?" The word *fucking* makes me flinch, like his anger is directed at me, though I know it's not.

"Yes, I'm fucking serious," I answer, and turn my face away.

Trees and gas stations tick by. The radio plays a guitar solo, a heavy backbeat. I wait for Matt to say more. His silence feels like condemnation.

"Are you sure?" he finally asks.

"What do you mean 'am I sure?'" I say. "I'm sure." Though a minute ago, I was already trying to rationalize it, excuse it myself.

"What is it you want me to do?" Matt asks as he accelerates, moving the truck into a passing lane.

My voice, which I'd put all my energy into maintaining for the service, cracks and breaks. "What do you mean 'want you to do?'"

I snap my head toward the passenger window. Greenhills is getting smaller behind us as we hurtle through the featureless land that separates the suburbs from downtown Houston. It feels as if there is nothing either of us can do. I need this job; we need me to keep this job. If I say anything about what the pastor did, I'm pretty sure that keeping my position will become impossible. He's important to the church, and I'm far less so. It's a year before #metoo, and my job won't survive an accusation against one of the most powerful men in the church. If I get fired we could lose our house. We're already walking a very thin financial line, and the chances of finding another job like this one are next to none. I'm not sure I would want to find another job like this one, at a church like this. But it's hard to think about what I want right now other than for my husband to display some sort of significant concern for me. Since he questioned whether or not I'm sure about what happened, he's been mostly silent.

"Can you say something, please?"

"What do you want me to say?" Matt asks, exasperated. He continues to look straight ahead, as I guess he must.

"If you were mine," the man I think I might love said, "I'd feed you." We were on the phone, one of the rare phone calls, and we were talking about my cough, about my allergies and the struggle with my voice. "I make great chicken soup," he said, laughter in his voice. I think of this snippet of a conversation, let it pass over me. *If you were mine.* Is this what I need? To belong to someone else? To be claimed, fed, plucked out of one existence and delivered into another?

It's been three months since we've spoken. I picked up a chip at my SLAA meeting, a round piece of emerald green plastic that marked how long I'd gone without him, like someone might celebrate the amount of time since a last drink, or a last hit of a drug. The green plastic chip looks like a piece from a board game or something you'd put in a slot machine. Not talking to him is something I should celebrate. When I picked up the chip, I felt proud of myself, proud that the dozen emails I'd written to him remained in a draft folder. I was proud that each time I'd wanted to call or text him, I hadn't. Instead I went to another meeting, itchy with withdrawal, and I talked about him. I listened to others talk about the people in their lives they were keeping away from, *one day at a time.* But after the pastor's unwanted touch, I don't care about the chip or the meetings or how long it's been since we last spoke. I need to talk to him. I want him to help me, fix me. I can hear the voice of my mother, something she said to me when I was a teenager: "Never depend on a man to take care of you." It was the early nineties and she was a working single mother, a feminist. I was raised to take care of myself, and yet I chose a religion, career, and life that insist on my dependence. I insist on it myself.

"I can't stand these people," Matt says finally, as we pass another strip mall and gray storm clouds gather in the sky.

"Who?" I ask.

"Church people," he says. "Every one of them. They're all just so full of shit."

I look at him, hoping he'll say more.

Anger rises in me. Why can't Matt react appropriately in this moment, be supportive in the way I need? And the pastor—it's unlikely I'll ever be able to hold him accountable. My anger expands to include every evangelical man I've ever worked for or with. Who has seen my body as less—less capable of leadership, less autonomous, less valuable in the eyes of God.

The Girl I Didn't Save

FEBRUARY 2011

"She's saying 'thank you' when she blinks like that," Hannah's mother says.

Hannah is dying. She lies in her bed, in her bedroom, surrounded by cards and flowers. Her mother sits on the edge of the bed, stroking her hand. Hannah's husband of one month is beside her, propped against pillows, cross-legged. A few close friends are here as well—they sit against the wall, knees pulled to chests, or lean against the window ledge. Every few seconds Hannah's ribcage rises in a struggle for breath.

Matt and I met Hannah three years after Budapest, while we were working for the young Baptist pastor at Koinonia. It was the first church we worked for with a congregation composed of people roughly our own age, and Hannah, twenty-seven, fit perfectly into its little galaxy of artists, lawyers, and school-teachers. She flitted easily between groups of friends, always smiling. The pastor often calls Hannah his favorite, but no one minds. Hannah is everyone's favorite.

In April, a surgeon cut a growth from her arm, a tumor she'd named Fred in an attempt to bring levity to the sit-uation. We'd been praying for her, getting updates on her surgery through emails, texts, and the blog she started. The pastor told the congregation about the good news from her doctor after the surgery—clear margins, no need for further treatment—and we let out a collective exhale. It felt like a bona fide miracle. We didn't say out loud that our prayers had healed Hannah because maybe we weren't sure. But we enthusiastically shared her story with unbelieving friends and family members as a testimony to God's faithfulness. Then we turned our attention elsewhere. Hannah began planning her wedding and imagining her future. In August, at her four-month checkup, her doctor told her, and she told us, that there was bad news. Rapid metastasis. It was in her lungs, and then it was everywhere.

When I got the text message earlier this morning from the pastor asking me to go and sing for Hannah, it had been a few weeks since I'd seen her. I am unprepared for how dra-matically her appearance has changed. Her head is smooth, bald as it had been, but absent the colorful scarf that's been part of her uniform since losing her thick chestnut hair. Hannah's pretty face is smooth too, no eyebrows or lashes. Her skin, all over her body, is gray. Her eyes are closed. Hannah's mother's hands lie lightly in her lap. I pull a chair from the desk and sit beside her.

"How are you?" I ask dumbly.

Her mother smiles and squeezes Hannah's hand. "We're glad you're here." ·

"Should we sing?" I ask.

I've begun to understand during my years as a music minister that in the time we spend with the ill and dying, through our songs and our prayers, we're supposed to be imploring God to intervene. We're constantly reminding ourselves, and maybe reminding God, that we believe God *can* intervene. No one ever uses the word *dying*, even if it's the correct word to use. We think this denial of the obvious, of the facts, is for Hannah's benefit—if we refuse to see how bad it is then maybe she won't see it either. But no one sees it or feels it more clearly than Hannah—we can sense that now. Our unspoken denials are actually for our own benefit. Hannah got sick, and then she got worse. Despite our prayers.

I pull my chair closer and silence my phone. The room is quiet. Hannah has adopted the firefly as a kind of spirit animal during her sickness and treatment, so fireflies in different forms—stuffed animals, ceramic figurines, drawings— are all over the room. The phrase she uses in her video blogs is pasted up as well: SHINE BRIGHT, FIREFLY. SHINE BRIGHT. Her video blogs have gone viral in the past few months, and the people around the world rooting for her, praying for her to be healed, have grown to near legion. Now, *Shine bright, firefly*—which at first represented hope for recovery, and then hope for remission—has begun to represent hope for a peaceful death.

It's unpopular at Koinonia to admit that one holds a child's view of God: a white-bearded old man with a clipboard, measurer of punishments and keeper of scores. Our God doesn't resemble that old God, the God of Abraham and Isaac, the God of the Old Testament. The historic God, the literary God. The God of our parents. Our evangelical

God is young. He looks much more like the young-man Jesus. He looks, more and more, though we don't admit this aloud, like the young man leading our church. White and Southern. Loving and pious. Somewhat conservative but cool. A God who would *lay down his life for his friends*, as Jesus did. Hannah is our friend, and though we can't literally exchange our lives for hers, we want to imitate Jesus in our care of her. If marrow or blood or a kidney was needed, one of us would readily offer. We would feel relieved to be able to help in a practical, tangible way. But Hannah doesn't need anything like that from us. We offer what we can: our presence and our prayers.

When Hannah could still walk, she came to the church for prayer. We huddled around her in the dark sanctuary, several ministers and many of her friends. We laid our hands on some part of her body—a shoulder, the top of her head—as we prayed and sang hymns. We asked the Holy Spirit to blow through the sanctuary, through Hannah's body and through each of us. We prayed that God would restore her body to the way we believed God had designed it, had intended it. We closed our eyes and tried to envision cancer cells being destroyed and healthy cells replacing them. Later, when Hannah could no longer walk, her husband carried her into the church—her head wrapped in that colorful scarf—where we repeated the same process. In December, she settled into a chair and said, "Christmas miracle?" and shrugged.

At that prayer gathering, what we called a *healing service*, one of the ministers told her that God had given him a message, that she would become a mother to several children. At the four-month checkup when the metastasis was discovered, her oncologist told her that there wasn't time to harvest her eggs; her cancer was too aggressive. If she survived, the doctor explained, her eggs would be too damaged from chemotherapy to give birth to a healthy child. The minister at the healing service didn't say his message was a metaphor. He didn't say that these children she would mother would be a part of her legacy as a teacher, sister, and friend. God had told him, he insisted, that her body would give birth. Her ravaged, weakening body. The minister had a Pentecostal background—a tradition that strongly believes in miraculous healings, healings on "this side of eternity." Though we doubted—silently, privately—we couldn't help but hope. Maybe he was right. Who were we to say? Hope was what we knew how to do.

It's February now, and Houston is cold and gray. Hannah's hospice attendant, a kind woman with noisy, colorful jewelry, is in the kitchen making coffee—I can hear the gentle metallic chime of her bracelets and the rush of the running water. I open my mouth to begin the first song, but my throat is tight and dry. If I cry, even a little, I won't be able to sing. I remember an old voice teacher warning me to always keep my emotions in check during a performance. "Crying closes up the throat," she warned. This isn't a performance, but I know that I'm here to allow Hannah's family access to their feelings, not to display my own. A clear bag of morphine drips steadily, and a catheter hangs beside the bed, the dark urine inside it streaked with blood.

O Lord my God, I sing, *when I, in awesome wonder, consider all the worlds Thy hands have made.* Hannah's mother joins me, and Hannah's husband too, for the second line. *I see the stars, I hear the rolling thunder, Thy power throughout the universe displayed.* My voice is steady, despite the dryness. I look at Hannah's husband, who sits beside her in the bed. I rest my hand on Hannah's, feel bones flutter under the thin skin like the blades of a fan.

As I finish, I remember that there's a bluesy gospel song that Hannah likes. It's a about climbing a mountain, even if you don't get to the top. As I sing, I think of the "you" in the song as God, asking the speaker to climb an unsummitable mountain. Hannah's cancer is an unsummitable mountain. On the other side of that mountain, the song promises—and so do I—that there is nothing but blue sky. Maybe even I have not yet accepted that the time to plead for healing has ended, if that had ever been a fair plea. If I'm not asking for healing with my song, with my prayers, then what am I asking for? Is comfort enough? I try not to look at Hannah's face as I sing. I focus on the fireflies, the cards, the headboard, the pattern on the quilt.

I think of Sabrina and her migraines in that room off Tompkins Square Park back in New York. Had my singing helped her? I wanted my singing to help, but I felt complicit in something that wasn't helping. What I'm doing now, singing the songs that remind us all of what we believe—that Hannah is headed to a safe place with no more tears, no more pain—motivates me. But what if. What if Hannah isn't going anywhere when she dies? What if when she closes her lovely eyes for the last time, she meets nothing? What if she meets absence, *death*? This is the first time I've allowed myself this level of doubt, allowed my mind to canter out into the field alone, without the leads of belief to reign it in. The shift that began in me in Budapest, where I'd questioned the belief that only the saved will make it into heaven, has brought me here, where I'm now questioning if heaven even exists at all. This shift feels heavier, and more consequential. It's one thing to question an aspect of theology; it's another to question the foundation of the faith. But the words of the songs I sing communicate a certain, unwavering faith, even if I can't. The sun begins to set, and I finish the last song. I hug Hannah's mother before quietly making my way out of her room, through the kitchen where the hospice attendant is reading a magazine, and out to the street to my car. I get a text message at five the next morning from the pastor, telling me Hannah is gone.

Later that same day, I get on an airplane to Ohio, where my father is having experimental heart surgery. My relationship with my father is strained, has always been strained. Since my conversion to Christianity, which he finds mildly perplexing, we've spoken just a few times a year. Usually a health problem he's having of one variety or another will inspire him to call. I'll offer to help, to do what I can from Texas. Once I flew to New Jersey to help him get through the aftermath of a particularly harrowing surgery. Then months went by with little or no contact between us, until he called me again, late at night when he'd had too much to drink. He was belligerent, wanting to rehash his failed marriage with my mother. This has happened several times over the years, and early in my Christianity, I would try to be loving and patient when he called. I would pray for him. I'd ask him to consider forgiving my mother; I would describe the forgiveness I believed God extended to everyone. I would also try to listen to my father's perspective on their marriage, something I would've never considered before my conversion. Eventually, my sense of obligation to hear him wore thin. The last time he called with a fresh tirade about my mother, I finally told him to stop. I told him not to call me again until he was ready to have a real conversation. We didn't speak for months after that, not until he called with news about this upcoming heart surgery. He would be flying to Cleveland from New Jersey, he said, even in his increasingly weak state, and he would need help navigating the hospital.

"Kyle will take me, fly me over there," he said, "and get me checked in if you can come for the second half."

The difficult half. The half that will include incontinence and confusion, breathing tubes and heart monitors. Kyle is my half brother, my father's firstborn son from his marriage to the woman he left for my mother. Kyle and I didn't grow up together, and we've always had a somewhat rocky relationship. But if Kyle can help, I thought, I should be able to as well. I'd been to Cleveland once before, in college when my boyfriend's band played a show at a dive bar. It was cold, that was all I remembered. In truth, I'd have preferred to stay in Houston with my friends, with Hannah's friends, to help organize her funeral. But my father needed me. He didn't usually ask for help directly. I bought a ticket to Cleveland.

My father didn't remarry after he and my mother split, but he's been in a relationship for nearly twenty years with a widow who lives in his town, the one where I grew up. I've never been sure if their relationship is romantic or simply based on the support she gives him: dinner every night, laundry, making sure he takes his pills and shows up to the VA hospital, where he gets his medical care. Why she isn't accompanying him to Cleveland, I don't know, but I can guess. I know how difficult he can be, how mean, especially when he's ill.

Shortly before we moved out of that town in New Jersey, when I was fourteen and my parents' divorce had been finalized, after the house sold and we packed up all our things, my father had a heart attack. It was minor, but it was painful and alarming enough for him to tell my mother about it, to ask for her help. Instead of calling an ambulance, she drove him to the hospital herself. With me and my younger brother in the back seat, she calmly pulled up to the curb in front of the emergency room and dropped him off. Not one of us said a word. He got out of the car, one hand protectively over his chest, and slammed the door. My mother pulled away from the curb, away from the hospital, the town, him, and the life we'd had there. Sometimes he reminded me of this during those late-night calls he made to me when he was drinking.

I apologized for it, many times, though of course I'd been too young to have any influence over how that event unfolded. I hoped my willingness to apologize would inspire him to do the same. *Look*, I was saying, *this is how it's done.* My faith dictated this; it gave me a template for uncoiling these hardwired hurts and grievances. Be humble, ask for forgiveness, then forgive.

My behavior didn't inspire my father to do the same. When our conversations reached that vulnerable place, it was always one-sided. I kept trying. I kept praying. I brought him up when prayer requests were taken at the Bible studies and small-group meetings I attended week after week. "This time it's to do with his kidneys," I'd say, or "It's his heart again." I was too shy to bring up the harder things, the emotional wounds. It was simpler to ask for prayers for physical healing. My friends were always eager to pray for him. They encouraged me to visit him, sent prayer lists around like chain letters with my father's Jewish name on them, which I thought he'd get a kick out of. I rarely mentioned to them the angry late-night phone calls I still got. Instead I focused the attention of my faithful friends on *healing* my father. What was even more important than healing his body was healing his soul.

"Do these people know you're Jewish?" he asked me a few years earlier, when I'd tried to give him a copy of the New Testament. He lay in a hospital bed then, recovering from another heart surgery, a valve replacement. The doctors had used a *porcine* valve, a pig's valve. It was a common surgery, one that others he knew had, but the non-kosher nature of implanting a piece of a pig's heart in his body made him pensive. Though he wasn't kosher, had never been kosher, there was a kind of dark poetry to the whole thing.

"Yes, they know I'm Jewish," I replied. He was silent.

"Pray with me," I said. I sat on the edge of his bed, on the thin cotton blanket, and held the copy of the New Testament I'd picked up while at the airport. It wasn't that my father's death was necessarily imminent, but that in order to have the courage to face him, I had to be the person I'd become. Not the old me—the girl at the top of the stairs who'd dared refuse his offer of a ride to a voice lesson. I had to be the new me, the minister. The Bible, the prayer, the language I used— it was all a part of that new person.

"And say what?" he asked gamely. "What would I say to God?" A yellow plastic water pitcher sat perspiring on the table beside his bed. The fluorescent overhead lights buzzed.

"Father God," I began, "I am a sinner." He was quiet. I continued. "I am sorry for the wrongs I've done…" I knew this part would be difficult, maybe impossible, for him. The only time he'd ever offered what could be construed as an apology was during his one brief stint in AA, when I was in college. He'd written me an "amends" letter, part of twelve-step recovery work. His apologies had to do with his drinking, though his letter was not specific. We hadn't seen each other in seven years then. After the divorce, I'd had no contact with him. But the letter surprised me. I hoped that maybe AA would help him to turn a corner. I finally agreed to see him in person, when I was home on winter break, and we made a date to have dinner. By the time the evening of our dinner arrived, my father was drinking again, his anger had returned, and the amends letter had been long forgotten.

"I believe you died for my sins," I continued. "I believe you rose from the dead so that I may have eternal life in you."

The words hung in the airless room. My father's hospital roommate shifted in his curtained bed; Fox News played on the television.

Part of me cringed at what I was doing, as I'd cringed in

Budapest leading Mark through this prayer, but I wanted my father to pray the Sinner's Prayer maybe more than I'd wanted much else.

"I invite you to come into my heart and my life so that—"

"I'm not ready for this," he said.

I looked at his large, red-rimmed eyes. His once-black hair had gone white and stuck out in puffs on either side of his head. I could see his bony shoulders beneath the thin hospital gown. At the time, I believed in the words of the prayer. I believed there were words powerful enough, if spoken in the correct order, to persuade God to accept a person no matter what they'd done before. I wanted God to accept my father. I believed that if he did, then my choices would have been right all along, even if my father and I never got our relationship right. If my father prayed this prayer, as I had, then nothing else, not what he'd done to me or I to him, would matter. All would be made new. His heart would give out, eventually, I knew. That mattered less.

"Pass me the remote," he barked, and pointed to the TV screen above my head. I set the Bible down.

Cleveland is as cold as I remember. Thick snow drifts pile on either side of the interstate, streaked with dirt and exhaust.

"It's lake effect," my taxi driver says, pointing at the heavy gray sky beyond his windshield. "Snow tonight." He frowns.

It has been so long since I've lived somewhere with snow, somewhere snow is a nuisance and not an ethereal wonder. I press my nose to the window as the taxi barrels along the highway and pull the collar of my coat up around my neck. I'm supposed to be sad now, carrying the mantle of this solemn trip and of Hannah's death, the anticipation of my father's condition. Yet I feel a kind of childish delight at the snow, delight to be on my own far from Houston. When the taxi driver pulls up in front of the hotel, I'm relieved to see it's within walking distance of the Cleveland Clinic, an elaborate, well-lit complex of glass, metal, and light. It looks like a city more than a hospital, or even like one of the light-spangled oil refineries south of Houston. I pay the driver and strap on my backpack.

"How many keys will you be needing?" the desk clerk asks as I drop my bags and unbutton my coat, sweating now in the blast of steam heat. He looks down at my driver's license. "Mrs. Hammon?"

I unzip my jacket and push my suitcase up against the counter with my foot. Will my father need a key? No, he's in ICU. Matt is at home with Sydney, planning Hannah's funeral. Who else would need a key?

"Just me," I say. "Just one." The lobby is empty. A fleet of coffee carafes sits on the far end of the check-in desk, and eighties pop music plays quietly over the PA system. The desk clerk runs my credit card and hands me the single electronic key.

I take the elevator up to my room and imagine the myriad reasons why women check into hotel rooms alone. It will be years before I meet the man I will become obsessed with, yet in this moment I think of what it would be like to be waiting for a lover in this hotel room, instead of waiting to see whether my father will survive surgery. It will also be years before I know that such thinking is a typical symptom of sex and love addiction—sexualizing feelings of grief, loss, or loneliness. The rush of seduction, even the rush of thinking about seduction, as anesthetic.

I slide my keycard into the door and toss my bags on the bed. Through the window I watch the last silvery light of the day disappear. I set down my backpack, lock the door, drag the desk chair up under the door handle, and pile the garbage bin on top of it. It isn't that I feel threatened; it's that I've become aware of my own sexual availability. I barricade the door to keep others out, and maybe, just as importantly, to keep myself in. Workers in orange vests four stories below sprinkle salt on walkways. New snow shimmers from the pitch-black sky. I exhale and stand in front of the window, stalling for just a few more minutes alone before what I know will be a plunge into the mania of my father's presence, his illness, the hospital.

"Where have you been?" he shouts. "Where have you *been?*" I stand beside my father's bed in the ICU on the cardio-vascular floor. Life-sustaining machines beep, buzz, ring an alarm. Nurses rush between curtained pods, not exactly rooms but more like holding bays, each one the temporary home of a patient in some state of delirium. Every light is turned up to full brightness. The slap of the therapeutic shoes against the linoleum, the thud of wheels on rolling beds, hydraulic arms being released, pushed back, modified. Patients shuttle by on gurneys, some motionless, with breathing tubes in their throats. Others thrash, like my father, like feverish children. A nurse leans over my father on his other side. "Mr. Dezen!" he says too loudly, as though he's shouting into a wind tunnel. "Your daughter is here to see you, Mr. Dezen!"

"Where have you been?" my father repeats, locking eyes with mine.

"I just got here, Dad, I'm staying at the—"

"What took you so long? *Jesusfuckingchrist* I'm here all by myself—"

"I'm here," I say, raising my voice and moving toward him. "I'm here—" A stab of guilt. What *has* taken me so long?

His eyes roll back. His hair is puffed out at the sides like it was the last time I saw him, only now it's thinner, whiter.

"He's just come off the ventilator," the nurse says. "He's still got the anesthesia in his system." He flips a switch on one of the machines tethered to my father's bed and adjusts the bag of clear liquid dripping into the IV in his arm.

"He's always like this," I say, forcing a half smile, trying to make a joke. The nurse circles the bed and leans down over his ear.

"Mr. Dezen!" he shouts again. "Your daughter is here to see you." Raw, chafed skin rims my father's mouth where the oxygen mask had been. Several drops of oxidizing blood, like rust-colored quarters, dot the blue hospital gown where someone, presumably the nurse, has made several attempts at finding a vein. The nurse leans back and looks at me. He's young, with short, light-brown hair and a tan despite it being February. The muscles in his arms and shoulders press out against his green cotton scrubs. He has several tattoos that are only partially hidden, though I can't make out what they are.

"Miss...?" he asks me.

"Dezen," I hear myself say, though I haven't used my maiden name in longer than I can remember.

"It may be a while before he comes out of this."

My father appears to have fallen back into a deep sleep, proving, I think, that his outburst was drug induced and not a part of some justifiable anger over how long it took me to arrive.

I want to ask the nurse a thousand questions—*Were you with him in surgery? Was the surgery successful? Why is he so combative? How should I handle him if he gets like that again?*—but I say nothing. The nurse is attractive, and I'm distracted. Mostly I want to keep him talking so he won't leave me alone with my father.

"Come back tomorrow," he says finally. "Tomorrow will be better."

Back in my hotel room, I open my laptop and find several email messages about Hannah's funeral. One of the other music ministers has written about Hannah's last few moments, including the words she said to her husband just before she entered a coma. "You have loved me so well," she said. In his email, the minister suggested that Matt and I write a song with that phrase, and that we could sing it at her funeral. I say the phrase aloud to myself. The TV is on mute, and the curtain over the large window is drawn. *You have loved me so well.* I close the email message and type Hannah's phrase into my computer, then several others. I write and delete phrases until I have a verse, and then a chorus. I call Matt and tell him I'll be emailing him lyrics for a song. Will he work on writing the music? This is our method of songwriting, though we've never done it while in different cities.

When I return the next day to the ICU, the nurse from the night before is nowhere to be found, and my father is asleep. I pull a stool away from the sink and wheel it over to his bed. The machines beside him hum and beep. I can't imagine how anyone could sleep with all this noise. Should I sing? And if I sing, what will I sing? I don't want the nurse to come by and find me singing—that would necessitate an explanation that would include what I do for a living, and I don't want to tell him that. Maybe I could sing something else, not a hymn but something my father would like. He loves show tunes, Broadway, big band stuff. The last time I saw him, he was very proud to recount his experience in a community theater production of *Kiss Me, Kate.* He launched into a bellowing chorus of "Luck Be a Lady" while his hospital roommate was lifted and turned by an orderly to prevent bedsores.

I decide to go down to the gift shop to see if I can find a CD of some music my father will like. He's sleeping heavily. I wheel the stool back to the sink and head for the elevator.

I return with an Ella Fitzgerald compilation album. My

father loves Ella Fitzgerald, and I've just gotten off the elevator when I hear a loud noise, a different kind of alarm going off. I don't know what it means or who it's for, but it reminds me of an alarm I heard once near the Upper West Side apartment where my mother, brother, and I lived after my parents' divorce. I was walking home from the subway when I heard it, and as I got closer to my house it got louder, though with each step I expected the opposite, for it to get softer, for the disaster to get farther away. The fire wasn't in my building, but it was too close for comfort. As I get closer to my father's bed, I have a similar sensation. I'm walking toward a disaster that isn't mine, a disaster I should be walking away from.

The nurse is there, shouting into my father's ear again, and several other nurses hover behind him.

"Mr. Dezen!" he says. "What can I do for you?"

One nurse adjusts the bag on the IV drip, and another takes his pulse.

"Get my salesman!" my father shouts. "Where is that kid?"

I stand as far away as I can while still being inside the curtained pod. No one notices I'm here, and I think about slipping out and heading back down to the lobby.

"Mr. Dezen! Are you in pain, Mr. Dezen? Are you uncomfort—"

"I need to talk to my salesman," my father repeats, in the tone of a prisoner of war trying to negotiate with his captors. Before I was born, my father had been what was called a *garmento*, a traveling salesman who represented American textile manufacturers to the fashion industry, a breed of Jewish man now long gone, evaporated after the business was shipped overseas. He spent a lot of time in department stores, and when he met my mother she was working as a buyer for one of the largest. He would later tell me that after they married—when, he believed, my mother was cheating on him with her boss—she developed such acute anxiety that she couldn't ride the escalator at work, though it was the only way to get from the sales floor to her office. My father believed her anxiety had to do with her guilt over the affair, or at least that's how he framed it when he told me that story. I know that sometimes patients with dementia can recall with utter clarity a time and place forty years in the past. He doesn't have dementia, but this outburst makes me wonder. It would be a cruel trick if he was stuck there, of all places, in his mind.

"I'm here, Mr. Dezen," the nurse says. "How can I help you?"

The alarm bells are silenced, and the other two nurses leave the pod, move on to other patients, more pressing needs. My father's eyes roll back in his head, and then close. The nurse turns to face me.

"I didn't see you there."

"Sorry," I say, though I don't know what I'm apologizing for.

"He'll be all right."

"What was that?"

"Sometimes older patients get ICU psychosis."

"He doesn't know where he is?" I have yet to have a lucid conversation with my father, and I am beginning to wonder if I'll be able to at all.

"It'll wear off in a day or so," the nurse says and starts to leave.

"I wanted to ask you," I start. *Do you want to have coffee with me? What are you doing later? Please don't leave me alone with him.*

He stands at the threshold of the pod, with one foot on the other side of the curtain. "Shoot," he says.

"Where's a good place to eat around here?" I ask.

I don't listen much to his answer. Instead, while he's speaking I'm deciding what I will do with the information. Will I ask him to join me? I finger my wedding ring, and I know what I must look like—bereft, lonely, making small talk, desperate.

"Let me know which one you end up at," he says, smiling, and leaves. His smile is clean. Not suggestive, not even coy. I look over at my father, who's now sleeping, and I wonder if the nurse thinks I'm behaving as a daughter would normally behave. Would a daughter who loved her father be more distraught? Would a daughter who loved her father be flirting with his ICU nurse? I'm relieved my father is asleep, though I'm not sure how long it will last. I pull the Ella Fitzgerald CD from my bag. It seems ridiculous now. I run my finger over the song list. My father's heart monitor beeps steadily.

He wakes up once more before I leave for the day, and I show him the CD. "Nice," he says weakly. I remind him of a conversation we had a few years ago, when Ella Fitzgerald was performing at Carnegie Hall. It was to be her last public performance, and as we talked, I fantasized about flying up to New York and taking him to the concert. I imagined us sitting elbow to elbow in the perfumed dark. That was the sort of thing I liked to imagine I would do with my father. I couldn't afford the concert tickets, or the plane tickets, and sensing that, maybe, he said, "Some other time." I was fairly certain there would be no other time, or times, so every time I spoke to him I forced myself to say, "I love you." Every time we spoke, since that day when I was child and we'd left him at the hospital, I thought it would be my last chance, and thinking ahead, I didn't want him to die without me having said "I love you." It had less to do with the feeling itself, maybe, than creating a seal against future grief. It was what I thought my future self, my future fatherless self, would want me to have said.

"I love you," I say. It's six o'clock, and a nurse has just brought him a tray of food. I hope he's finally settling down. "I love you too, honey," he says.

Over the days that follow, he has several more outbursts, a few of them directed at me. I cry in the ladies' room more than once. Though I see him through the worst of his recovery, I feel, for the first time since my conversion, that no song, no prayer, no petition will change a thing about his illness, or about anyone's illness. Just like nothing would change my father. Not my love or my lack of love. Not my effort or my lack of effort. The new person I have become is not new enough. I think fiercely about the nurse—his tattoos, his hair. I imagine us walking together. Meeting for coffee, talking. I begin to talk to him in my head. In my fantasy he mostly listens but pauses to say, "You're a good daughter, Cameron." Instead of going out to look for the nurse, I finish writing the song for Hannah and call my husband.

"I've got to get out of here," I say. I try to cry, to underscore the urgency to Matt, to convince him that buying a new plane ticket, one that would get me home a few days early, is worth the expense. I can't cry. I worry what I might do if I don't get home soon.

"What about your father?" Matt asks.

"I just can't do this anymore," I reply.

The next morning, I get on a plane to Houston. I'll see my father once more, after he's diagnosed with stage four colon cancer. I'll spend that visit in a similar mix of hope and hurt, alternately praying and griping about his temper, his unpredictability. When he passes away, alone in a nursing home, I won't have seen him in almost two years. I imagine I will carry the guilt of that, and the grief, not only for his death but for our relationship, for what it was and what it could've been, for the rest of my life.

I've heard it said that a person gets her idea about God

from her father. When we prayed aloud at Koinonia we so often said, "Father God," at the beginning of every petition, as we had when we'd prayed for Hannah. I knew early on that I would have to get rid of my idea that God was anything like my father, but in the end, it turned out to be easier to get rid of my father. To move to the other side of the country, to put as much distance as I could between us. To call him only rarely, and to rarely take his calls. To see him infrequently. Only then, I thought, could God have a fighting chance of becoming God's self in my mind, and not a poor replica of an imperfect man. But my strategy failed. It felt as though nothing I did, or could do, would make a difference—to God, or to my father. It's not that I really expected my father to become kinder, to become more like a father to me, least of all due to something I'd done. But I allowed myself to hope that some wrongs would be made right.

The Thing Itself

Later the week of the fundraising service, the week of the assault, I meet Fi at a coffee shop that hosts a rotating art show by local painters and sculptors. Fi and I don't know each other well yet, so while we drink our coffees under the brightly colored canvases, we talk about our families, mine in New York, hers in Ireland. We talk about our jobs. Fi is a homeopath, which she explains is a system of alternative medicine based on the premise that a small amount of what causes symptoms of an illness in a healthy person can heal those same symptoms in someone who's sick. There's a poetry to this I admire. Fi tells me that she left the movie business many years ago—where she'd worked for that Irish film director—after getting sober from alcohol, and her career in alternative medicine followed. Though the desire to finish a screenplay she's working on remains, she has a growing client base who seek her out for her powerful remedies and, I imagine, for her equally powerful wisdom. I know she treats several women from SLAA. One of them, a woman I've grown close to who suffers from MS, was so inspired by the success of Fi's remedies that she decided to quit her job and go to school to become a homeopath herself.

When it's my turn to talk about my work, I'm nervous. Because Fi is gay, I worry that knowing what I do for a living—working for an evangelical church—will make her wary, distrustful of me. I wouldn't fault her for it. The anti-LGBTQ crusade is a shameful hallmark of evangelicalism. Many evangelical leaders and pastors have made it their life's work to push gay Christians out of the church. The pastor from the Refuge, for example, is known nationwide for his rejection of gay marriage and refusal to recognize the ordination of gay clergy. His public campaign calling on all evangelicals to do the same has amassed a following. Though there are also evangelical ministers who *don't* believe gay Christians should be excluded, who perform clandestine gay weddings and bemoan the church's harmful policies to their few like-minded friends, they are a mostly silent minority. The pressures of the culture are too great, as is the long-held and dangerous belief that the right amount of prayer and willpower could simply reverse a person's sexual orientation.

I don't ascribe to this prejudice and never have, but I also don't openly challenge it. As I believed about my support of women in leadership roles in the church, I likewise thought if I quietly loved gay people and supported their rights while being inside an environment that feared and maligned them, maybe I could be a part of changing that belief. Several of the ministers I know who work for megachurches and secretly perform gay marriages hope it will be only a matter of time before these policies are overturned. I haven't been alone in my mostly naive hopes, but as I sit across the table from Fi, I begin to feel the weight, and the cost, of my naivete.

My only other close gay friend in recent years is a man I met shortly before he willingly went to a seminar at a local church that was designed to help him to stop being gay. When I was growing up in and around New York and working in the fashion business, most of the men who were close to my family, and close to me, were gay men. After becoming a music minister in mostly evangelical churches I lost touch with them, and quickly figured out that gay men and women, at least those who are out, don't attend the churches where I work, churches that don't affirm them. In the years that follow, this fact and my silence about it will bring me a sense of deep shame and regret, one I was only just beginning to reckon with when I met Fi.

My friend who went to that seminar had grown up in a family of committed and active members of one of the biggest Southern Baptist congregations in the country, and Southern Baptists categorically *condemn homosexuality as sin.* Though he'd been living most of his adult life as an out gay man, he'd decided—maybe out of a sense of social or familial pressure, maybe out of a genuine desire—that he wanted to marry a woman and have children. I told him I supported him no matter what, and he seemed to be genuinely happy when he did meet a woman and fall in love. Later, when they had children and the birth announcement arrived in my mailbox, I felt conflicted, unsure if his friendship with me had helped or hindered him in figuring out the life he wanted for himself. I wished that my friend had felt he could be both a gay man and a Christian, that he could be a gay Christian man with a family. But I hadn't offered that possibility to him during our many conversations, during the times we'd prayed together. The version of Christianity that he and I both subscribed to at that time didn't allow for it, and we didn't know there was any other version of Christianity. Not yet. Our mutual Christian friends—those who'd been praying that he would be "healed"—saw his transformation as evidence of God's *will*, God's intervention. His other friends, friends from the art and design world who'd known him before he took that seminar, thought he'd lost his mind.

Sitting in the coffee shop in front of Fi now, I feel the familiar anxiety of trying to hide this complicated legacy of the community I've built my life around, and of my complicity in that community, trying to translate this increasingly untranslatable part of my life.

"What is it that you do, Cameron?" Fi asks.

"I'm a music minister," I say.

"A what?" Fi's accent blows air into the *w* and *h* like wind in a sail.

"I arrange and perform sacred music for church services."

This term, *sacred music*, is one I've taken to using lately. In my mind it suggests organs and choirs, not rock bands and smoke machines. Perhaps it brings to mind a church with the progressive worldview of some higher, or more formal, liturgical denominations. *Sacred music* might describe choir hymns at Westminster, an orchestral performance at the Vatican, or the chanting of a dirge by Orthodox monks. Sacred music is, at least to my mind, an elevated enough concept to separate the music from its religious content, allowing it to be experienced on its own merit. I hope that this definition I offer Fi is enough. I hope I won't have to describe what it is I actually do: sing Jesus-is-my-boyfriend–themed pop songs to often-wary, suburban evangelicals, under a half-a-million-dollar sound-and-light system.

"Sacred music?" Fi smiles. "Well, that's lovely, Cameron."

While Fi cuts into a pastry, I talk about how my schedule affords me a lot of free time to work on my own writing and music. I describe how flexible the Refuge is, how little they ask of me.

"It's such a tiny fraction of what you're capable of, though, Cameron. Isn't it?" she says.

I'm not sure if the question is rhetorical. I haven't thought of it like this before, of its limits. I haven't thought that there could be more or should be more. That I want more. Not since trying to make it as a musician in the secular world, anyway. I've also not allowed myself—not really—to look at the fact that by virtue of standing on the stage at the Refuge I am actively endorsing its worldview, a worldview that harms people, that hinges on exclusion. Up until now, the good I believed I was doing had been worth the trade-off. But when I tell Fi about the Refuge, about the kind of church it is, I can see the hurt and surprise in her face, and it feels like a trade-off that has long outlived its usefulness.

"It's a bit avoidant?" Fi asks. "The job, I mean."

I'll come to understand and appreciate that Fi has a way of saying very pointed things, things I need to hear, by phrasing them as a question.

"Avoidant? Ah," I say. "Yeah," remembering a conversation we'd had the week before, in the courtyard of the old church after an SLAA meeting.

"Emotional avoidance," Fi reminds me. "You give so little of yourself, but you also get so little back."

During that conversation, Fi and I had talked about how protecting ourselves from failure, romantically and professionally, might keep us safe, but it also keeps us stuck. We'd talked about how Fi realized that, in her darker, love-addicted moments, she'd avoided real emotional connection with her partner and sought it instead where it was dangerous—and ultimately unavailable. With someone who was a fantasy. This pattern left her always wanting, never fulfilled. I could relate. It is, after all, what I'm doing with the man I think I might love.

Living in my head, in a fantasy, is actually something I've done all my life. I'm always waiting for something, it seems. I even wrote a song about it not long after my baptism. *Wait in me, and I will wait in you.* I turned my willingness to withstand something unfulfilling into a spiritual discipline. There are, actually, religious precedents for this idea. The Israelites of the Old Testament waited, wandering in the desert for forty years before making it to the Promised Land. Jacob waited seven years (and one week) to marry Rachel. Jesus of Nazareth waited forty days in the desert, withstanding the Devil's temptation. These were the stories I heard in church, stories that I grasped hungrily. But most of the waiting I was doing in my own life was not about withstanding temptation; it was about protecting myself from taking any real risks. It was avoidant, and the waiting kept me passive.

"It's a big one for me," Fi says. "I've got to ask for what I need. Or else it'll all go to shit." She smiles.

That night, I spend longer than usual with Sydney, worried that my preoccupations are keeping me from giving her the attention she needs. We take our time doing her going-to-bed routine, the brushing of teeth and the locating of her special blanket and stuffed animal. We read a story together and pray, a slightly altered call-and-response version of the Prayer of Saint Francis, as we do every night. This prayer is not one I've ever heard used in evangelical circles. I picked it up from a Catholic writer I'm reading. In her book, she prays this prayer with her young son, and though I'm giving little credence to the idea that anyone or anything is listening, the ritual is comforting to me, like a lullaby.

"Make me an instrument of Thy—" I begin.

"*Peace*," Syd answers. She burrows beneath her hot-pink comforter.

"Where there is hurting—"

"Let us show *healing*."

"Where there is doubt—" I say.

"Let us show *faith*."

"Where there is division—"

"Let us show *unity*," Sydney says.

"Oh, Divine Master," we say in unison, "grant that we may not so much seek to be loved but to love, to be understood, but to understand, for it is in giving that we receive, it is in pardoning that we are pardoned, and it is in dying to self that we are born into eternal life." Syd's eyes are wide in the dark. "Amen." A helicopter is flying low over the city, rattling the glass in her bedroom window.

"Stay with me, Mommy," she says, and reaches for my hand. I don't know if she's scared or just wants to delay her bedtime. I have a hard time reading her these days. I worry that I'm losing her, that she's drifting from childhood to preadolescence and I'm missing it, too distracted. I lie down between her and her life-size teddy bear, an old Christmas gift from my mother.

"What's the matter, babe?"

"It sounds so close," she says, thrusting her chin in the direction of the window.

"It's probably a life flight," I offer. She knows about life flights from the local firemen who came to talk to her class. "They're taking someone to the hospital, babe, for help. It's a good thing." In the past we would've prayed together for whomever was in that helicopter. Now it seems inauthentic to pray like that, to instruct Sydney to pray like that—the sort of intercessory prayer I first learned by singing for Sabrina—when I'm not sure what I even believe about that kind of prayer anymore. The Prayer of Saint Francis is about as much as I feel capable of saying with sincerity.

"Someone must really be hurting right now," she says softly to herself.

This takes my breath away. Someone really *is* hurting right now. She's hurting, and I'm hurting. I bet if I looked hard enough, I could see that Matt is hurting too. I don't see my part in it, though, not clearly. I don't see how everything I do and don't do—every inflection of my voice, every time I turn away and stare into the middle distance while Sydney or Matt is talking, every time I take far longer than I should to answer a simple question—I don't think about how this hurts them. I'm too lost inside myself to notice.

"You're right," I say. "I bet someone is hurting right now."

I lean over her forehead and press my lips to her warm skin. Though she's eight, I can still detect a remnant of that baby smell, the warmth that radiated from her when she was an infant.

When I finally climb into bed with Matt, I turn to the wall and pull the covers around me tightly. Matt and I haven't spoken about the pastor and what happened backstage at the Refuge since that tense exchange six weeks ago in the car. I suppose it seems pointless to bring it up when we both know there's nothing that either one of us is willing to do about it. I won't report the pastor, not for years, because I'm fairly certain I'll lose my job if I do. Why won't Matt confront him? For the same reason, I guess, but it still hurts. We've slipped back into the roles of co-parents and roommates, speaking only to arrange a play date or dinner or swim practice for

Sydney. I try not to wake Matt up, and I'm relieved that he's already snoring. I remain very still, until the familiar pattern of his breathing puts me to sleep too.

The next morning, while Matt is at work and Sydney at school, I email the man. It's been four months since we've spoken. I saw online that he'd had a painting accepted to a gallery show, so I send him a message, breaking my own rules. "Congratulations," I write. "I want nothing but good things for you." I wait a day for his reply, refreshing my email again and again. I'm surprised by how quickly I'm consumed by the need for a response. I make bargains with myself—if I don't hear from him within twenty-four hours I'll block his number, his email, his social-media profiles. Then I think— *he shouldn't respond to me; that's the right thing to do.* When this thought crosses my mind, I'm jealous of what I perceive as his advantage over me.

While I wait, I stare at my piano, and at the blank piece of paper on the music rack, presumably for the song I'm going to write. A line comes to mind, and I struggle to fit it over a simple chord progression. The lyric is cardboard, opaque. I cross it out and start over. Sunlight comes in through the backdoor window and lengthens over the piano. My phone buzzes with a text message. It's from a number with the area code of his city by the sea. "Finally," I say aloud. There's no name attached to this number in my contacts, but the message contains a picture. It's of the title page of a book I love, *Bluets*, a collection of prose poems by Maggie Nelson. TO CAMERON, the inscription reads. GREAT MEETING YOU. I've never met Maggie Nelson, but I told the man about this book that night at the arts conference, before he walked me home in the dark.

"I went to her reading at a bookstore here," he writes. "I got drunk."

"Hi," I reply. "I've missed you."

"I wanted her to sign this for you, a gift. But she got confused and thought I was you."

I laugh. I see my reflection in the black lacquered front board of my piano. "Thank you," I write. "I must have this."

"Then you must see me."

Bluets is about a failed affair and the color blue. I love the book because the narrator is negotiating erotic and spiritual bewilderment through the numbered fragments that make up the narrative. Blue is the color of religious adulation—the Virgin's gown, the sky-blue background of religious paintings—but it's also shorthand for pornography, as in blue films. The interwovenness of these desires, religious and romantic, and the way the color captures both, captivate me. At the time I read it, I hadn't yet met the man, but maybe I knew somehow that I would, that this experience was waiting for me.

During the months when the man and I weren't speaking, when I briefly gave my social-media passwords to Fi so I wouldn't be tempted to look, and then begged her to give them back to me, he'd read *Bluets*. He'll tell me later that for weeks he posted pictures that corresponded to its individual numbered sections. I was supposed to see the number on the image, and then go read that section in *Bluets*. "2. And so I fell in love with a color…as if falling under a spell, a spell I fought to stay under and get out from under, in turns." This was how he worked around my refusal to speak to him, my vow of "no contact," by developing a coded language using my favorite book, by posting these messages, poems, and song lyrics, making me look for clues on social media. I'd meant it when I told him we couldn't talk. I'd meant it in the sense that I knew if we continued my resistance would break down. We would consummate this, and there would be

no going back from that, at least for me. When he'd posted
those pictures, I'd been staying close to Fi, close to my SLAA
meetings. I wasn't looking for messages from him then, but
I'm looking now. I sit at my piano texting him, my prior res-
olutions disregarded. I don't care about the boundaries I'm
breaking, the promises I've made to myself and others. I'm
relieved that I can begin feeling something other than the
grinding anticipation of the past few months.

The messages go back and forth all afternoon. He tells me
that he thinks the affair depicted in *Bluets* took place over
three years, and that's what he wants for us. "Three years
sounds like a long time to be in pain," I answer. But three
years is better than no years, I think. It's something. I'm so
sick that I'm willing to accept this—*crumbs*. In SLAA, when
someone is utterly fixated on getting what they think they
need, they'll settle for tiny fragments of attention and affection. It's never enough, of course, but we tell ourselves whatever we need to in the moment to keep going: He loves me.
He'll change his mind.

It's unlikely he'll ever change his mind, the man I think I
might love, or any other person who qualified someone to
enter into recovery for sex and love addiction. It's also unlikely that what he feels for me and I for him is *love*, but I can't
see that yet. In the early days of my conversion, I followed
the breadcrumb trail, the signs from God I saw in the world.
It's a different trail of crumbs I'm following now—of pictures
posted, of poems, and of lyrics. I don't say what I really want
to say to him—*Why not forever? Why don't you want me forever?*

Soon it's time for me to go pick up Sydney from school,
and text him goodbye, break the spell, return to my life.

"Can we talk again later?" he writes, "or tomorrow?"

"Yes," I reply. "Please." We do talk again the next day, and
the next. I stop going to my weekly meeting. I stop seeing

Fi. I don't tell anyone that we're in contact again, not even my therapist. It's been six months since I was with the man, since I was in his physical presence. This is only the third time we've spoken since then. How willing I am to shut everything else out.

I got a tattoo on my ribcage a few years earlier—*the thing itself*—a line from "Diving into the Wreck" by Adrienne Rich:

> It is easy to forget
> what I came for
> ....
> the wreck and not the story of the wreck
> the thing itself and not the myth.

It was a few months before I quit my job at Koinonia, when I began to realize I was losing the pale pulse of what I came to the church for. The business of God had obscured God. Much like, perhaps, the business of marriage had obscured love. After years of struggling to catch, and recatch, that pulse, God now seems to me like the headlight on a sinking ship, weak and getting weaker.

Women in my meeting talk about making a person, a lover, into a god. When so much of a person is colonized, overtaken like this, the object of the obsession can become a kind of deity. Once the man and I start again, we're always talking. I sneak off to the grocery store parking lot to text or call him, I pull my car over to the shoulder, or ditch a meeting or lunch date. Even when I'm not talking to him, I'm talking to him. Passing shop windows filled with things I would never wear, I try to picture myself in them. Floral sundresses, floppy hats, bangles. Things I think he might like, some version of me he might prefer. In a store at the mall: *Would he like this on me?* In front of my closet as I dress for the day: *Would he like this color? This fabric? This cut?* When I read something, when I can focus long enough to read: *What would he think of this?* Back in New York, I was talking to God in my head all day. This is what Sabrina had told me to do: "Talk to God like you would to a friend, but in your head." This is what it means to *pray without ceasing*, a command Christians all over the world take from what is likely Saint Paul's oldest letter in the New Testament. Talking to the man in my head all day is a kind of prayer. A prayer to a person with no power but what I give to him. And I give him much. When I'm talking to him in my head, the pastor's hand on my body, Matt's silence, my growing discomfort in my role as a minister and with the idea of calling myself a Christian, and my sense that my daughter is slipping away from me—all of these things are obliterated. The way the pop from a flash whitewashes the photograph.

There are moments when an awareness settles on me, and I realize that I'm building something out of nothing. But then I remind myself that not-nothing happened between us. *Not-nothing*, a compound. It wasn't *nothing* that happened, but was it something? Falling in love with someone you cannot or do not see, someone invisible, is a lot like falling in love with God. The love object is always at a remove. What happened between God and me, signs, *tongues*, voices, the messages found in dreams, in weather—this was a kind of not-nothing. If any of it had really happened anywhere other than in my head, who could say? People build worlds around an invisible God, go to war, carve and dismantle civilizations. Or move across the country, trade one life for another, as I did. Maybe invisible love, at least for me, makes sense. Maybe it's the kind of love I understand best.

The next day, I text him again. I remind him of the summer arts conference I've signed up for, that in a matter of months I'll be within driving distance of him. *Will we or won't we is* too tiresome and frustrating. In my mind, this is not about sex. What certainly began as lust, as bone-deep hunger, has become something else. I want a deeper communion.

"Will I see you?" I write.

He doesn't reply.

Phoenix

That night, while I wait for him to respond to my message, I get ready for the last in a series of creative writing classes I've been teaching at the Refuge. I print essays, dog-ear the craft books I'll use, go over my notes. A dozen women from the church, and from the surrounding communities, show up to my class, faithfully, each week. Because my interaction with the congregation at the Refuge is limited, as I've designed it to be, I was surprised when the women's minister asked me to teach this class. Most of the staff didn't know that I had interests and aspirations outside of religious life, but word about a writing class I'd taught downtown had gotten around, and they asked me to offer it to church members. Maybe, I thought, there was a way to integrate who I wanted to be with who the church thought I was.

Over the course of our twelve-week class, each woman has written and shared her true stories—of illness, of spiritual doubt, of childbirth, divorce, loss. I've been surprised by how deep they're willing to go, and how generous they are with one another. I don't want to show up unprepared; I value them. But it's hard to focus; my lesson outline and notes are a blur. When I finally do sleep, I dream about the man. He says, *I have a plan.* I hear the simple words in his voice. I wake up flooded with relief. With the comforting sense that he will give me what I want. That his answer to my question will be the answer I need.

Years ago, a few months after my baptism on Coney Island, I'd had an HIV test and was awaiting the results. I didn't really think I had HIV, but I'd just been diagnosed with the STD that had propelled me toward conversion with a kind of near-death urgency. I got the HIV test because I wanted to start my new Christian life with a clean slate, something Sabrina had urged me to do. The night before the test results came in, I dreamed that I was on the road with my band, and we were touring a beautiful city where we would be performing that night. Our guide took us to a walking bridge that overlooked the glassy rivers and lush parks. The tall buildings shimmered, gold and silver, side by side. The warm afternoon sun shone in a clear blue sky. "Next time we'll have to stay," I said to the guide, urging us on to conclude the tour, conscious that we had somewhere to be, that our time in this place was limited. When I told Sabrina about my dream, she pointed me to a chapter in the book of Revelation, the last book of the Bible, which describes heaven as a place where "the street of the city was pure gold, as it were transparent glass." I'd never read Revelation, but the dream had calmed my fears, and I took it to mean that when I did die, even if it was from HIV, I would go to this shining city. I had nothing to fear from death. Death had *lost its sting*, like the ancient Jewish prophet Hosea predicted, a sentiment repeated in the New Testament by Saint Paul. Belief in a resurrected Lord, and thus in all believers' eventual rising, is meant to make Christians fearless in the face of death. It explains why so many Christian martyrs went to their deaths singing. I was a long way from that kind of faith, but the dream imparted a sort of preternatural calm, the same calm I'd seen on Sabrina's face and the faces of the other women who bravely waded into the Atlantic for my baptism. The test results had come back negative, and my anxiety had been suspended. By the time I was baptized, I'd already begun to believe that dreams could bear messages worth deciphering—messages from God even. Some residue of that oneiric faith made me trust my dreams of the man.

In the large, sunny classroom at the Refuge where my workshop is held, my students read each other's essays, offer praise and gentle criticism. While they do, I check my phone for a message from the man. We've planned to talk after I'm done teaching, to make a plan for seeing each other at the arts conference. I'm still filled with the calm of my dream, but I'm checking my messages anyway.

"Sometimes getting what we want is the fastest way to learning what we really need," Susan, a seventy-year-old grandmother, says. She finishes reading the passage from her essay to the class, and while they offer feedback, I turn her phrase over in my mind. Aphorisms are a big part of Southern communication, and I find them tricky to comprehend for the most part, especially because the ones I hear in Texas draw on a host of shared experiences that still feel alien to me. But this one: What do I want? What do I need? Two questions that haunt me lately. When Susan's workshop time concludes, the women begin unpacking cupcakes, cookies, and drinks. We're celebrating the work that they, and we, have done. I take a picture of the maple cupcake one of the students brought especially for me, and I post it to social media. I'm proud of this, that they've liked my class enough to buy my favorite cupcake. It's a small thing, but it feels like I'm finally developing something I love and am good at, outside of singing in church.

By the time I climb into my car for the long drive home, my good feelings have evaporated, and my body is bracing for the coming phone conversation. I've unhooked myself from the buoy that's been keeping me afloat for the past eight months. I haven't been to an SLAA meeting or talked to Fi in weeks. I don't want to lie to her, or to the other friends I've met there, and I don't want to let them down. We hold each other up, but we also hold each other accountable. I don't want to hear what they will surely tell me, either directly or with their silence. That I have to let him go. *No contact.*

"I had a dream about you last night," I say when he finally calls, as I'm pulling into my driveway, gravel crunching under my tires.

"Did you?"

"It was a good dream. You had the answer for all this."

I turn my key in the lock and push open the front door, balancing the phone between my ear and shoulder. Matt is at work, at a new job at a local high school. Sydney is at school. The house is empty, dark, and quiet.

"I can't do this," he says. "We can't do this."

I put my purse down gently, lean my backpack up against the bookshelf. I'm quiet, trying to hear him clearly.

"What do you mean?" I say. "Can't do what?"

"I've thought of it a thousand ways. It won't work," he says.

"We'll have to change our social media habits," he continues. "I'm not going to quit it, I need it for my art, but let's try not to get caught in each other's feedback loop. And if you're going to that conference I won't—"

"Stop," I say. "You're talking about social media?"

He continues to talk about the ways in which we'll need to detangle from each other. He's thought this through, prepared his speech.

"We can't be friends," he says. "Maybe in two or three years, but not before that." I'm too surprised by my sobs to be embarrassed by them. It feels like they're coming from someone else. Finally, I stop crying.

"I'm not leaving you," he says. "Do you understand that I'm not leaving you?"

I don't know what that means. "Say goodbye," I say.

"Goodbye."

I press the round red button on the screen of my iPhone. I go to my phone's settings and block his number. He did have the answer after all; my dream was right. I don't know yet to be thankful. I don't know yet that this is mercy.

That night, once Matt and Sydney are home, after I've quickly made them dinner, I climb into my car and head to a meeting. I'm wearing the metal pendant of a bird around my neck that a friend gave me for my birthday last year. When I tell Fi what's happened, that it's finally over, she points to my necklace. It's a phoenix, a supernatural bird from Greek mythology that rises from the ashes, again and again, a parallel to the resurrection story of Jesus. I finger my necklace, eyes puffy from crying, and shrug at Fi. I'm not rising from anything, not yet.

This Is My Body

JUNE 2016

"Take, eat: This is my Body, which is given for you…"

The priest holds the wafer over his head as he recites the familiar words. I hear the faint snap as he breaks the wafer in two and lowers his hands over the silver tray. I'm standing behind him, in front of the microphone, watching him bless the elements for communion. I'm at St. Mark's, the Episcopal church, singing for the jazzy 5 p.m. service I do every week.

The body and blood are different everywhere. Holy Immanuel used soft Hawaiian bread straight out of the plastic wrap. They filled the metal cup with grape juice as congregants lined up to "rip and dip." Tribe, the charismatic ones, the ones who prayed in tongues, stacked rice crackers and offered tiny paper cups of cheap wine. No one chewed, no one wanted to risk getting Jesus stuck in their teeth. We swallowed the crackers whole, handled the cups in meaty fingers, and tossed back the liquid like a shot.

"Take and drink: This is my Blood, poured out for you..."

The priest lifts the decanter of wine and pours it into the chalice. The congregation slowly rises from the wooden pews and begins to stretch out in a single line toward the priest, toward the bread and wine.

St. Mark's is candlelit tonight, and the warm lights that hang in the arched cross beams are turned down low. The words of the liturgy—"to you all hearts are open, all desires known," "in your infinite love, you made us for yourself"— feel serious. Or maybe it's me who's serious. I feel very different than I did last summer, when I was preoccupied with the man I might have loved. As then, we're not in contact, but this time I'm really listening to the words of the liturgy. What does it mean to break one's body? What does it mean to break one's body for someone else?

When I was pregnant with Sydney, I had the sense that my body was being hijacked, being taken over by a hungry life force. The steady buildup of blood and tissue culminated in a harrowing birth. After twelve hours of labor my doctor rushed me into surgery, sliced just above my pubic bone, and pulled her out, blue and silent as a stone. Moments later, she was crying, my doctor exhaled, and all was well. But the crash from the pregnancy hormones, a crash I hadn't expected, triggered the postpartum anxiety that no amount of praying could cure. When I became pregnant again three years later, I was terrified I would go through all that again. But six weeks into the pregnancy, the familiar hormonal buildup abruptly stopped. My tender breasts deflated. My appetite waned. I chatted nervously to the technician who drew my blood, filled tube after tube to the brim. My doctor promised the tests would be easy, painless, but I knew nothing about being a woman is painless. I took communion the Sunday morning before the Monday blood tests and ultrasound. The pastor preached on the Gospel of Timothy that day. *She will be saved through childbearing*, he read.

The ultrasound confirmed that my pregnancy wasn't viable, but my body already knew. I gave Matt the ultrasound picture. *This is my body*, I thought. I held my thumb over the motionless white orb. *This is my blood.* I told Matt to throw the picture away, to get rid of it. I'd wanted to forget, but I never stopped carrying that grief. He put the picture in the back of his sock drawer instead, and it stayed there for years.

Matt gently strums the familiar chords to the hymn on his acoustic guitar as each person walks forward, holds out their hands for the wafer, then lifts the heavy silver cup to their lips. I step forward, move my lips to the microphone, and close my eyes. *O Lord my God, when I, in awesome wonder, consider all the worlds Thy hands have made.*

As I sing, I understand that Matt is also carrying grief. I was too afraid to look for it. Maybe his silence and distance were about his disappointment with the church, his own pain over the miscarriage. He turned it in on himself, as I knew him to do in our first few boozy years together. I look at him, so focused on his playing, possessed by the music, eyes closed.

Matt's eyes open and meet mine. This, here, is one world, a world without the phantom lover I thought could save me. My husband is real. He's flesh and blood and standing beside me despite everything—despite the grief we've suffered together and the grief I've brought on us. He's still playing his guitar, filling the sanctuary with the music that moves my lips to sing, moves the congregation to sing. My body knows that I've entered this world, the world with my husband, my daughter, and my life in it. My mind is slowly catching up.

After the congregation returns to their seats, and we've sung the last notes of the song, we speak in unison—

Almighty and everliving God,
we thank you for feeding us with the spiritual food
of the most precious Body and Blood;
and for assuring us in these holy mysteries—
Send us now into the world in peace, and grant us
strength and courage to love
and serve you
with gladness and singleness of heart.

A few days later I arrange with my therapist to invite Matt to one of our sessions. I'm too afraid to tell him alone. I'm afraid of his anger, and of his lack of anger. I'm afraid he'll leave me, and I'm afraid that he won't. I'm afraid, irrationally perhaps, that he won't let me see our daughter, that he'll take her away from me. Even though I could never imagine taking Sydney away from Matt, my mind provides me with every possible scenario.

I haven't wanted to tell Matt until now because I believed that unburdening myself at his expense was cruel and unnecessary. Maybe also because I wasn't ready to let the man I might have loved go. I haven't told Matt yet because the story didn't have an ending. It has an ending now. No matter what happens from here forward, no matter what Matt decides, he deserves to know who I am and what I've done. How else can he make a fair decision about whether or not he wants to be with me? Maybe love without honesty is only sentiment. Matt deserves more than sentiment and so do I. "Nothing changes if nothing changes," we say in SLAA meetings.

I've started going to meetings again, returning sheepishly, listening mostly. Before the meeting with the therapist, I text Fi, "Help." I text another friend from SLAA, and another.

They all remind me that I'll survive the telling. Matt will survive. There is no way past this but through.

I sit on the too-deep couch as sunlight streams through the windows. By some strange coincidence, my therapist's office backs up to the garden where Matt and I were married thirteen years ago. The owners of the garden have sold it, and in a few months the azaleas and bougainvillea will be dug up, the fountain dismantled, and the bricks hauled off to make way for a luxury apartment building. As I sit and wait for Matt, I watch landscapers dutifully digging and weeding, planting and pruning. Steps behind them I stood, a slip of a girl in a white dress, a new Christian, newly moved from New York to Houston. I stood and promised to be faithful. Not just to Matt but also to the life we were building together. I promised, we both did, to *forsake all others*. And here I am now, anticipating the moment in which I tell him that I've failed. Not only have I failed to be faithful in my body; I've failed to be faithful in my mind, in my spirit. I imagined another life and was willing to trade this one for the other. I take a sip from my water bottle. Matt knocks lightly on the office door.

"Come in," my therapist says. She's tall with short, dark-blond hair. She crosses her legs and drinks her coffee.

Matt walks in sweating. I've told him only that we need to talk, that we need to address the tension between us, and that I think my therapist can help mediate that conversation. He lowers himself uneasily onto the loveseat, as far from me as possible, and crosses his ankle over his knee. The school year has just ended, so he's retired his teacher's uniform of button-downs and jeans and is wearing shorts. He's pale. He looks tired. My therapist leans forward in her chair and motions for me to start.

"I wanted to invite you here," I say, as I'd rehearsed in my head, "because there's something I need to tell you." I say that I met someone, a man. I tell him that I had feelings for this man, and that our feelings became physical. My words feel wooden, heavy.

"We didn't—have sex," I stammer. As though what we did hadn't put me under a spell, a spell I fought *to stay under and get out from under, in turns.* "I thought I had real feelings for him," I say. "I believed I did."

I might still have real feelings for him, but I'm beginning to understand that feelings pass, like weather. Some weather reshapes rocks and cliffs, causes streams and rivers to escape their banks and flood the streets. Other weather only lingers for a while, and then is gone.

"What did you do?" His voice is loud, and his cheeks are flushed.

I've prepared for this question. I asked my therapist if she thought he needed to know all the details. I didn't want to give him images to picture in his mind.

"I don't feel comfortable answering that question yet," I say stiffly.

"When will you feel comfortable answering it?" he snaps back.

"Do you want to be with this person?" Matt asks. He exhales and crosses his arms over his chest, sinking deeper into the couch.

"No," I answer. "I don't." He doesn't say anything. "I've been lonely," I say, "for a long time. I know that doesn't make this okay."

"No, it doesn't make it okay," he says. I can see his eyes are filling with tears.

"I was wrong, it was wrong. I know that. I just—I don't know what to say. I fucked up."

He doesn't respond.

"This will take time," my therapist says. The buzz of a

plane overhead mixes with the drone of the leaf blower from the other side of the window.

"I'm sorry," I say. "I am." For everything that's brought us to this moment.

"What do you want me to say, Cameron? What do you want?" This is familiar. He asked me this in the car after the pastor touched me backstage at the Refuge. Now, as then, I don't have an answer.

For two days Matt avoids me. He stays out of the house for as long as he can, and when he returns home he's gruff, distant. I go to meetings. I organize the utensil drawer in the kitchen. I vacuum my car. I have no expectation of what Matt will do. On the third day, I arrange for Sydney to spend the night at a friend's house, and Matt and I meet at a nearby restaurant for dinner. He's less tense than he has been, but we still haven't spoken about what I told him in the therapist's office.

"I don't want to be angry," he says, the overpriced plates of food between us cooling. "I don't want to carry this around. I don't want to be that person."

"Okay," I say.

"If I believe what I say I believe about love and faith, if it isn't all bullshit, then my love for you has to be bigger than this. *Is* bigger than this."

I hope he'll say more. I can't remember him saying this much about anything in a long time.

"I love you," he says, and reaches for my hand. "We're going to be okay."

We begin to talk about what happened to me backstage at the Refuge, and the way Matt's tepid reaction had made me feel. "I was afraid that if I let myself get angry, if I allowed myself to really feel that anger, that I'd do something I'd regret."

"Okay," I say, "I get that. But I needed you then, and you were unavailable—you'd checked out."

"I'm sorry," he says. "I'm such an asshole. I hate that I made you feel that way. I'm going to do better."

I begin to cry. I don't want to cry in this restaurant. I'd told myself that I would be okay either way, with Matt or without him. That I'd understand if we couldn't get past all of this, if he couldn't stay with me. But that was only partially true. I've loved Matt since I met him. Since before God. Before faith and doubt, and transgression. I don't want to be without him. I would survive if he left me, maybe even thrive, but I love him. Our daughter loves him. We're a family. A stronger family than the one I grew up in ever was. My love for Matt and his for me, for who we are together and who we could be, is enough.

Thirty days after the confession, I'm getting ready for that arts conference up north when I get a call from the young, tattooed pastor who is technically my boss at the Refuge. I've taken the week off from my job there, hired another singer to fill in and lead the band, but the pastor wants to meet me downtown, at a new coffee shop. "No," he says on the phone, "it can't wait until you're back from the conference." I'm surprised he wants to drive all this way, surprised by his urgency. I'd been unsure about going to the conference in part because my father's health had taken a turn for the worse; he's dying, and the window of opportunity to see him again is closing. My trepidation was also due in part to the man I'd worked not to contact. We hadn't spoken since that last goodbye, but he lived within driving distance of the conference, and though I felt strong, I was wary. The pastor had been surprisingly amenable to my taking the time off. I'd registered for the conference, bought my plane tickets, done a mountain of laundry, and was ready to go.

I arrive at the coffee shop, on the main drag of Montrose, Houston's traditionally gay, artsy neighborhood. The tattooed pastor is already there. He's standing in front of the big, east-facing window, and I can see he has a poorly applied spray tan that looks orange in the daylight. His long hair is gathered in a loose ponytail. He wears a short-sleeved button-down shirt tucked into khaki pants. Musicians, students, and artists sit at the bistro tables, crouch behind battered laptops, taking advantage of the free coffee refills and strong Wi-Fi—evidence of Houston's thriving gig economy. The pastor looks out of place in this coffee shop. He looks out of place in his own skin. He's telling several conflicting stories without even opening his mouth.

"What I'm about to say isn't easy," he begins as soon as I sit down.

"It isn't?" I ask, smiling, trying to make light of the dramatic tone he's taking.

Things have been tense for me at the Refuge since the incident with the pastor, though I haven't told anyone about it. Another coworker, a fill-in guitar player I didn't know well, was aggressive with me a few weeks later. ("Are you trying to shake my hand?" I asked when he leaned in awkwardly. "No," he answered, "I'm trying to punch you in the face.") I reported it to the church's human resources director, but nothing came of it.

"We're going in a new direction with the Refuge," he says.

"We are?" I say. He's silent. "What direction is that?" I ask.

"A direction without you."

It's my turn to be silent. I shouldn't be surprised, but I am. I think of my plane ticket to the conference. Of the money I suddenly shouldn't be spending. I search the pastor's face to try to make sense of what he's just said. I think of the brakes my car needs, the fact that our mortgage payment is due in a few days.

"So you're going to fire the girl and see if that helps," I say, remembering the pressure he's been under since he arrived to grow the church's attendance.

"Yes," he answers, then hesitates, maybe thinking over the legality of firing someone based on her gender. "Yes, basically." Though churches are bound by the same anti-discrimination laws as all businesses are, the practice of hiring and firing ministers is an exception.

I'd been so afraid that I would be found out, that my obsession with the man would surface and cause me to lose my job. I'd been afraid that telling the truth about the pastor would cause me to lose my job. In the end, my female body, the fact of its existence and what it asked of the men around me—to allow themselves to be led, to be taught by me—was too much. The pastor says that the church needs a more aggressive musical style at the Refuge, something closer to what a man can offer, what the male bodybuilder who'd had the job before me offered. It's because I'm a woman. Not a sinful or adulterous woman. Just a woman.

I'll later learn that it was a secret committee of laypeople, all women, who made the decision to fire me. Many of those women came from Southern Baptist or other conservative denominational backgrounds that believe women shouldn't lead, that it isn't biblical. They wouldn't support me just for the sake of supporting a woman in church leadership, regardless of whether or not they liked my style of music. It's a sort of Stockholm syndrome, the willingness of evangelical women to uphold the system that represses them. I've done my fair share of upholding that system. It's that willingness in me—and in other women—that keeps the system afloat. I've made a career from it. Until now.

Though I'm surprised, perhaps mostly by the pastor's honesty, I'm also relieved. Fi would say this is God doing for me what I could not do for myself. If I believe in this God, I might really get a hold of this phrase, understand it. Or maybe my belief is not paramount. As I sit across the table from the pastor, who rubs his forehead, what I get a hold of is that I will never again have to stand on the stage in that blue-lit room as fake smoke pours from a dry-ice machine.

Then Sings My Soul
(Two Agnostics Walk into a Coffee Shop)

NOVEMBER 2016

I smell the cool air on Fi's gold puffer jacket. Her cheeks are ruddy from her three-block scooter ride. She's a jovial presence in Montrose, zipping around on her Vespa, blue eyes sparkling, her shock of short blond hair bobbing as she navigates the wide, tree-lined streets. I get up to hug her, and then we sit across from each other at the same table we sit at each time we meet.

"What is there to say but how are you surviving?" she asks, wincing.

It's been four months since I told Matt, four months of us living in a new reality. And it's been four weeks since my father died. Despite my grief, I want to tell Fi that I'm okay. I'm handling it better than I was at first. Fi doesn't know how hard it's been because I haven't told her. I've been isolating, keeping to myself.

When I went back to New Jersey after my father's death, to help my brothers empty my father's apartment, I got an email from the man I thought I might've loved. It landed in a junk folder because I'd blocked him months before, but I'd been checking that folder anyway, almost unconsciously.

Before my father died, Matt and I had been making our way back to each other. *Let me help you with that?* as I yanked a stuck closet door or struggled with the top of the peanut butter jar. Or *How are you feeling today?* apropos of nothing. He was asking me questions, seeing me. *You're so beautiful,* he'd say while I squinted at the crow's-feet like shattered glass around my eyes. Though I'd shrug off his offers of help, and his compliments, I needed him to say those things.

When I got the email, it had been almost a year since I'd last spoken to the man. I'd been going to meetings. Singing at St. Mark's on Sunday nights, praying my wobbly prayers. I'd been making the daily and sometimes reluctant choice to mutter "thank you" or "help" into my coffee cup, or before falling asleep at night, choices that led me away from despair and toward hope. My father's death upended that tentative peace. I couldn't pray, or mutter-pray. I couldn't get out of bed. *I've been left again, by my father,* I thought, self-pityingly. *And I've been left by the man I might've loved.* This is the story I told myself, despite all the progress with Matt. His email was polite and short, two sentences, but it reopened something. I composed response after response and filed them, unsent. It was a familiar pattern, talking to him in my head all day long. Writing emails I'd never send.

I went to SLAA meetings and talked about how I was white-knuckling it, that I was unsure if I was going to be able to survive losing my father and all it was bringing up for me without restarting old habits. A few women nodded as I spoke, and a few others reached out to me with text messages or emails to say they'd been through something similar. They encouraged me to keep coming back to meetings. To stay focused on my recovery. Grief is a common trigger, they said, not only for sex and love addicts but for all sorts of addictive behaviors. Even though I knew this, I wanted to talk to the man. I wanted to know if I might love him still.

When a few weeks of this wanting had passed with no sign that it would let up, I made an appointment with my therapist. "You don't talk about God much," she remarked as I sat across from her in her new, sunny, blue-painted office. "As a tool," she continued. "You don't talk much about using God as a tool."

I squirmed. God again. Higher power. Something greater than ourselves.

She was right that I hadn't been talking about God much. I'd set God aside. "I've been a professional religious person for more than a decade," I said. "You'd think I'd have the God part down."

She laughed. "I don't know if it's ever something you *get down*. Thinking of God like a tool might help lift some of the baggage."

"I don't know if I can believe it anymore. The God that I believed in with Tribe, and then at Koinonia, even in Budapest. I don't think I know that God anymore."

"What if you've just outgrown that God?" she asked. "What if there's still something for you to grow toward?"

"I want to understand myself. Can that be enough?" I picked at my cuticle.

"Maybe," she answered, smiling. "But I think you should try it. Just to see."

During my time in SLAA I'd been focusing more closely

on the parts of my dysfunction that I thought I could understand and control. After so many years in religious communities where psychiatry and psychology were frowned upon, the idea of trying to understand my own psyche felt liberating, rebellious almost. In truth, it wasn't working, which is why I was back in my therapist's office. I'd educated myself, reading books and blogs, going to meetings and talking to others in recovery. When I talked to people who seemed to have really experienced healing, though, they had a spiritual practice, a spiritual connection. Some took regular morning walks, *walking meditations*, they called them. Some read poetry. Some prayed the Psalms. Some did yoga. I did none of those things. I'd say the serenity prayer, but only when I was desperate. I said it silently to myself, as I'd been taught to do in meetings. When I said the words I was temporarily relieved, distracted. It calmed me down, as I suppose it's meant to, but I didn't think of it as a spiritual practice.

I've been drifting farther and farther away from any sense of belief, and any connection to God. I've allowed myself to entertain the idea that maybe God wasn't real. How can I stay connected—really connected—to a fairy tale that I've potentially outgrown?

Since I was fired from the Refuge, I'm not working full time at a church for the first time in a decade. Though I'm still at St. Mark's, I've protected my heart from getting too invested there. There's no pastor in my life these days to build a false notion of God upon. I may have outgrown *that* God, but I have not yet set about rebuilding a notion of God in any meaningful way. I'm unsure I know how to. It takes a long time and a lot of energy to let go of faith, and perhaps just as long to rebuild it. I'm not at the rebuilding stage yet, and I'm not sure I'll ever be. I do know that if I force it, it will fall apart again. Back to the beginning.

While I was in New Jersey to collect my father's ashes and close up his apartment, I made the choice to stay with Kate, an old friend from college who lived in a converted farmhouse with her young family. Otherwise, I would have had to ping-pong back and forth between my mother's apartment in Manhattan and my father's in New Jersey, between my mother's complicated grief and my own.

Once my plane landed in New York, I hopped on a commuter train and soon found myself at Kate's kitchen table on an autumn day, deep in the woods, surrounded by hills and trees, by miles of golden leaves that fluttered like prayer flags along the two-lane road that led to her house. We talked easily, like no time had passed. I told her about my spiritual rudderlessness. About how since I'd allowed myself to doubt Christianity, I'd found it impossible to return to the confidence of belief.

When we'd been close in college, Kate and I were both a little lost, both pulled between boyfriends and potential boyfriends, between booze and schoolwork. It seemed to me, sitting at her table, that we'd reacted to those early years in similar ways. She became a doctor, and I became a minister. Repairing people was a focus of both our lives. Had we repaired ourselves? Could we? Kate had stopped drinking years ago, and she still went to meetings. She believed in a higher power. She believed it kept her sober.

"I know I have to get this part right, the God part," I said. "To heal. I have to. But I can't grasp it."

"My first concept of God, my first *higher power*, was the sound of Johnny Cash's voice," Kate said, swiveling on the wooden chair at her kitchen counter. "And the smell of my grandmother's cold cream."

We'd spent many long-ago drunken nights singing along with Johnny Cash and Patsy Cline records, but I'd never thought of something like that—a smell, a sound—as being divine. As being God itself, or a part of God, or a way toward God.

"I think *higher power* and my mind snaps shut," I replied, rubbing my eyes. The light above her stovetop buzzed. The woods were now dark, and I couldn't see anything beyond the windows, just our reflections.

"Johnny Cash," Kate repeated, shaking a pale strand of hair from her eyes. "Cold cream."

For weeks after, I thought about what Kate had said and tried to put it into the context of my own life. Perhaps my first sense of God had been the smell of winter on my father's wool coat when I was a child. The feeling of his beard tickling my cheek as he kissed me. The faint smell of cigarettes and alcohol on his breath. Maybe later my sense of God had come in the dream I'd had before my baptism, the comfort of the calm sea.

Mystics through the ages have made it their work to find ways to God. To find and inhabit the right conditions that might render a person receptive to even the smallest fragments of the divine. Fractured bits of experience, memory, beauty that open into something larger. Saint John of the Cross is famous for having entered the dark night of the soul, a deep, isolated time of meditation in order to move away from the known world—of eating and drinking and living and dying—and toward the unknown world. The liminal, spiritual world. For Saint John that way was the way of darkness, and maybe it was for me too.

I tell Fi about my time with Kate, about Johnny Cash and cold cream.

"When my dad was admitted to the nursing home I thought of a story my mom told me, about when I was born," I say. "It was one of the few good stories she had about him.

He stood outside her hospital room when she was having me, and paced. He kept watch, and when I was born, finally, he passed out cigars to all the doctors and nurses. It was a kind of vigil," I say. "When he was sick in the nursing home, unable to walk without help, waiting to die—would I do that same thing for him? I kept a vigil for many people. I sang for Hannah, and for others who were dying. Would I do that for my own father? I didn't. In the end."

Fi listens, nodding. Her hair catches the white winter light. She runs her finger along the rim of her mug. The PA system in the coffee shop plays a Stevie Wonder song.

"As I'm sitting here, I'm thinking of the strangest thing," Fi says, "and this may sound insane, but I'm thinking that maybe no one has ever done that for you. Maybe no one has sung like that for *you?*"

I've never been on the receiving end of the kind of singing Fi's talking about, the kind I'd learned to do at Big Hug with Tribe when I'd sung over Sabrina. Fi's statement seems the truest thing anyone has ever said to me.

"I can't carry a tune," she says, "not at all. But I'm going to sing for you, and maybe you'll hate this song. It's a *Christian* song, I think," she says. She shrugs. "Maybe you'll hate it."

"Maybe I'll know it," I offer, and smile.

Her cheeks flush. She straightens, inhales, and quietly, steadily, begins to sing. I don't look over her shoulder at the man sitting behind her who was hunched over a laptop but is now looking in our direction. Or at the barista who's lingering at the counter over a drink she's already poured. Instead, I focus on Fi's mouth forming the words.

O Lord my God, Fi sings, *when I, in awesome wonder, consider all the worlds Thy hands have made, I see the stars, I hear the rolling thunder, Thy power throughout the universe displayed. Then sings my soul, my Savior, God, to Thee. How great Thou art.* She pauses.

"This is for your dad," she says, and sings, *How great thou art*, pointing a long, dancerlike finger at an empty spot beside our table, as though someone—my father? his ghost? God?— is standing there. "And this is for you," she says, and swivels her finger toward me. She sings the chorus again.

Of course Fi has no idea that this song is one I sing almost every Sunday. The one I sang for Hannah, one I've sung for years. It's the song that we've worked up into a New Orleans second line–style celebration at St. Mark's, where the priests process out of the church, marching and swaying up the aisle to the sound of the jazz pianist soloing over the chords. The congregation sings and claps. They smile. I smile. That song is so much a part of my life. I've sung it for dying people, yes, but I've also sung it for people very much living. Maybe I'm one of those living people.

"Here's what I do," Fi says, after she's finished singing. "I ask what I don't believe in—" she pauses to make sure I'm following, "to help me to believe what I don't believe."

I repeat her words back slowly. She's saying that I should ask what I don't believe in—in this case, God—to help me believe *in* God. If there is a God, I think, it seems reasonable that it would take some kind of movement on God's part to wade through all my many layers of doubt, to reach me in my unbelief. This is a small act of faith—to ask what I don't believe in to help me believe.

"It's so clear to me," Fi says, "that you're marinating in spirit. Whether you believe it or not, it's part of who you are." She laughs. "It's like a fish not believing in water." Though I haven't known Fi long, she seems to know me in what feel like the most important ways. She knows that I'm God-haunted and always will be.

I imagine myself in that marinating water, in the cold Atlantic off Coney Island where I waded, so eager to be changed. I look around in the water, in the murk, and I see the ghostlike passage of fish. I see an oar, a rudder. Is this my testimony? The smell of a wool coat in winter. A melody, a lyric. Initials in a license plate. A small collection of the numinous, like shells on the beach still wet from the sea.

Epilogue: Mystery

It's been just over a year since Matt and I sat in view of the garden where we were married and I told him the truth. It's July, and we've come to the Pacific Northwest on a rare vacation. In the rental car, we barrel across the Hawthorne Bridge on our way out of Portland to the mountains. Driving together is part of our history. Inside a car, moving at high speed through one city or another—this is where we seem to understand ourselves and each other. Maybe because a car is a neutral space—and a road trip, any road trip, is an act of hope. We're moving together toward something new. I turn up the volume on the song we're listening to so it reaches deafening, and fold my hand over his. It's awkward because he keeps raising his hand to flick the turn signal, or pick up his coffee, but when he rests his hand again on the gearshift, I settle mine on top of it.

When I told Matt about the man I might've loved, he absorbed what I told him like certain marine life absorbs oil after a spill. He took it into himself. He let it work its way in and through him. But it didn't kill him, or us. It made him glow, in a way. More precisely, it made parts of him glow that I'd never seen before. Unlike his reaction when I told him about the pastor's assault, when he deflected, let it bounce off of him, asking me to tell him what to do with it, what to say. This is different. This is not invisible love, the sort of love I feared I understood best. This love is a verb.

It's not easy; it's not perfect. There is still so much work to do, not only between us but between me and the church, between me and my ideas about who or what I can be in the world. My ideas about God. The work is ongoing, and it falters sometimes. Between Matt and me this work looks a lot like talking. Saying "I need you now. I need you to hold me, to hear me, to see me." It's not easy for me to say those things to Matt, or for him to say them to me. We fail a lot. But we keep trying, every day.

Between me and the church, this work is about not looking away. It involves speaking and writing about what can and must change inside churches where abuse and inequity flourish. It involves seeking out churches that affirm and celebrate women, people of color, and the LGBTQ community. Churches willing to be transparent about their doctrines and policies. Willing to stand up for love, justice, and equality, all the time—not just when it's convenient for them.

Between God and me, this work looks like allowing myself to experience God. In the sound of Johnny Cash's voice, in a memory from my childhood, even if to do so is considered heretical to the evangelical communities where I once belonged. I'm learning to let go of my tight hold of religious narratives, but to also allow myself back into them when I choose to. After my father died, I asked the priest at St. Mark's to insert his name into the prayers we say each week for members of the community who've died. I stood up in a pew and wept while his name was called, and I felt a deep and abiding gratitude for this faith tradition that I'm a part of, even though I wrestle with every aspect of it, still. Belief is mercurial; faith is something deeper. It's the faith part I'm working toward, and I imagine I will always be working toward it.

As I look out of the passenger window at the Willamette River, churning and lapping, a dorsal fin breaks the froth, glints in the summer sun. The water conceals some mystery, has the power to change landscapes.

Acknowledgments

You hold this book in your hands because a small cohort of extraordinary women took a chance on me and then worked tirelessly to make sure my story was born into the world. I am deeply grateful to my agent and friend Amanda Annis, my publisher Emily Smith and editor Beth Staples, and Anna Lena Phillips Bell—for vision, asking the absolute right questions with kindness, and never letting me get away with anything; and to Morgan Davis for making one of the most important introductions of my life. From my heart, thank you.

Thank you to the Publishing Lab at UNC Wilmington and everyone at Lookout Books, past and present, especially Nicholl Paratore, Tyler Anne Whichard, Katherine O'Hara, Lindsay Lake, Nikki Kroushl, Cassie Mannes Murray, Michael Ramos, Kate Barber, Kinzy Janssen, and Caitlin Taylor.

Profound thanks to Robert Gottlieb and Trident Media Group.

Thank you to Lauren Winner for lighting the way and for being a true mentor and friend.

To my teachers Paula Huston, Greg Wolfe, Jim Daniels, Tom Feigelson, Steve Almond, and Joni Tevis, my gratitude and admiration, always.

My thanks to Christian Wiman for generous permission to use his words as the epigraph to this book.

To Nick Flynn, Naomi Shihab Nye, Jessica Wilbanks, Angela Morales, and Scott Erickson for beautiful endorsements, and for inspiring me with your art.

To my dear friend Lacy M. Johnson for seeing me, knowing I could do this before I did, and for the best advice, always; to Lindsey Kidd, no words describe how much I love you and how grateful I am for your friendship—thank you for being with me through it all; Lauren Donelson for spiritual sisterhood and the portal; Fi Connors for book midwifery and life-changing wisdom; Chris Cander being willing to answer every emergency text with love and read every emergency draft; Mark Haber and Tobey Forney for being my literary life raft; Bryan Bliss for a hand up; Kate Aberger for many important conversations at kitchen tables and many more, I hope, to come; Alison Wisdom for friendship on the journey; Jamie Quatro for trailblazing and generosity; Randon Billings Noble for listening to this book as an idea and encouraging me to try it; Tina Richardson for that first, critical push, and many after; Anna Sneed, for more than a decade of friendship and beautiful pictures; my beloved Pleiades and MFA cohort—Kaitlin Barker Davis, Hannah Piecuch, Colleen Dawson, Kate Schifani, Mary Bergida, Betsy Brown, and Joanna Campbell; Patrick Miller and St. Mark's Episcopal for being sanctuary when I needed it; and Tribe, for modeling faith with integrity and being my first spiritual home. To Stu Shelby for well-timed wisdom; Luke Brawner for bringing *The Ish* to life; Kim Thompson and Brené Brown for believing in my voice and giving me the chance to use it. To Amber Bollinger—thank you for loving my brother (and me) so well, and for being the coolest person at every family gathering.

Big thanks to Writers in the Schools Houston, Inprint

Houston, Writespace, everyone at Brazos Bookstore, especially Ülrika Moats; Lance Cleland, Nanci McCloskey, Lisa Metrikin, and everyone at the Tin House summer workshop 2016; and Matt Leone and the Colgate Writers' Conference. Thank you to the Collegeville Institute, especially Kirsten Linford, Josina Guess, Carla Durand, and Don Ottenhoff; and to the Glen West Workshop and the Master of Fine Arts in Creative Writing Program at Seattle Pacific University.

Thank you to the Binders, the village that kept me sane, informed, and challenged, and without whom this road wouldn't have been nearly as fun.

I am grateful to the editors of *Ecotone*, the *Butter*, the *Literary Review*, *Gigantic Sequins*, *Image Journal*'s *Good Letters* blog, *Killing the Buddha*, the *Houston Chronicle*, and *Catapult* for publishing the essays that haunted the writing of this book, and for giving my work a home.

For my family: Mom & Alex—we did it. Three little heads bobbing in the ocean. I love you so much. Thank you for always believing in me.

In memory, Dominick Callo & Howard Dezen—I miss you. I hope I've made you proud.

To the Lovings, with gratitude—David, Patty, Mandy, and Maya; Jerry and Cathy; Cameron and Don House, Mary Cameron, David, Jack, and Charlie.

To the Hammons, Bill and Paula, Billy, Ava, and Mary, for being the family I chose.

Finally, to Matt & Sydney, you are my heart. You are my everything. This is for you.

Cover photograph © Deb Schwedhelm.
Cover design by Emily Louise Smith; interior design
by Tyler Anne Whichard; and composition by
Nikki Kroushl, Lindsay Lake, Cassie Mannes Murray,
and Katherine O'Hara for The Publishing Laboratory,
University of North Carolina Wilmington.

TEXT LTC GOUDY OLDSTYLE PRO 10.5 / 14.7
DISPLAY RALEWAY LIGHT 20

Lookout Books

Lookout is more than a name—it's our
publishing philosophy. Founded as the
literary imprint of the Department of
Creative Writing at the University of
North Carolina Wilmington, Lookout
publishes books by emerging and
historically underrepresented voices,
as well as overlooked gems by established
writers. In a publishing landscape
increasingly indifferent to literary
innovation, Lookout offers a haven
for books that matter.